Storied Recipes

short-short (true) stories & the recipes that flavor them

Contributed by the members & friends of SOMOS

(Society of the Muse of the Southwest – "the literary heart of Taos")

Edited by Bonnie Lee Black

Taos, New Mexico

Society of the Muse of the Southwest

P. O. Box 3225, 233D Paseo del Pueblo Sur

Taos, New Mexico 87571

575 758 0081

www.somostaos.org

somos@somostaos.org

SOMOS is funded in part by New Mexico Arts, a Division of the Office of Cultural Affairs; the National Endowment for the Arts; the Virginia Wellington Cabot Foundation; Healy Foundation; and Taos County Lodgers Tax. *Storied Recipes* is funded by individual sponsorship.

This project was made possible by the efforts of the 2012 SOMOS Board; Linda Michel-Cassidy; executive director, Dori Vinella; SOMOS staff; Rebecca Lenzini of Nighthawk Press, Taos; and the generous support of the writers and cooks who contributed to it.

ISBN 978-1478397519

First Edition

Edited by Bonnie Lee Black

Production Manager: Lorraine Lener Ciancio

Copyright 2012 by SOMOS

Recipes and stories used with kind permission from the authors

Cover photograph by Geraint Smith

Interior photographs by Dan Cassidy; pages 91, 191 by L.L. Ciancio; page 210 by Bonnie Lee Black

Designed by Lesley Cox, Feel Design Associates

SOMOS

The Literary Heart of Taos

Editor's Foreword

One theory explaining why cookbooks sell well, even in today's wobbly economy, is this: They're read in bed. It's not as though all those cookbook buyers are avid home cooks; most, in fact, are more like dreamers. Cozily horizontal beneath a quilt, they turn the pages of a delectably designed cookbook—kept not in the kitchen, where it might get stained, but safely on the bedside table—and fantasize about a life that would allow them to do more cooking and entertaining at home: More leisure time, a bigger food budget, better knife skills, limitless kitchen equipment, matching dinnerware... Mostly, though, they dream of more time and money. Cookbooks are storybooks for grownups.

Acting on this theory, we've compiled a cookbook filled with short, true, well-crafted stories—and the recipes that flavor them—as a fundraiser for SOMOS, Taos's own literary nonprofit organization. We cast a wide net in our call for submissions and were delighted with our catch. Taos, after all, is a town teeming with creative types; so fishing for creative talent here is particularly effortless. Just put the word out, and reel the responses in. Our *Storied Recipes*, then, is a showcase for the talents of the many friends of SOMOS—storytellers of all stripes who love to cook as well as eat.

We were particularly struck by the breadth of the submissions we received. Stories poured in from men and women, young and old; poets, playwrights, novelists, biographers, memoirists, and all the rest; lifetime Taoseños and more recent arrivals. And the stories themselves, some funny, some poignant and nostalgic, span the globe—from London to Venice, from Africa to Qatar, from Greece to New Zealand (with a heavy dollop of Italy in between).

Our contributors generously share their memories and recipes from earlier lives lived elsewhere in this country, such as Shoo-Fly Pie from Pennsylvania, Chicken an' Dumplin's from the Deep South, and Anadama Bread from New England. The recipes, too, range from the sublime (a caviar recipe handed down from a real Russian prince; a stuffed-clam recipe served on Millicent Rogers' grandfather's yacht) to the humble (tuna casserole, of which we offer two) to the practical (a fail-proof high-altitude cake recipe, which alone is worth the price of this book). Some of the recipes are tributes to friends; many (no surprise) are homages to grandmas.

In his introduction to the 2009 edition of Brillat-Savarin's classic *The Physiology of Taste* (translated by M.F.K. Fisher), Bill Buford wrote about "the charisma of food, its capacity to be everything":

It is identity, and culture, and history. It is science, and nature, and botany. It is the earth. It is our family, our philosophy, our past. It is the most important matter in our lives. It is more than its ingredients. It is transcendent.... But it is also just dinner.... It is serious, and not.

Storied Recipes, in its own slim way, illustrates this kind of charisma. Its stories speak of identity, culture, history, and family. It is meant to be serious and also not. For example, among its contributor-tested recipes are one for chiles rellenos that takes three months to make (to grow the chiles) and another for elk stew that calls for a game hunter.

So the recipes, you'll find, are more than just their ingredients. But do try them. Yes, take this book into the kitchen and cook something from it from time to time. Most of all, though, think of the stories as bedtime snacks. Keep *Storied Recipes* on your night table and savor it in bed.

Bonnie Lee Black

2

President's Letter

SOMOS, the Society of the Muse of the Southwest, is a nonprofit literary organization based in the culturally diverse town of Taos, New Mexico. SOMOS has existed for thirty years. This alone is an amazing accomplishment for any organization; but for a nonprofit, it's almost a miracle. So what accounts for our longevity?

To begin with, SOMOS is an organization that reaches far beyond its borders to create a plethora of programs for and about writers. Throughout the calendar year, curators put together events and programs like the Winter and Summer Writers' Series that bring in established local, national, and international authors to read their work and lead workshops.

In addition, every autumn SOMOS presents the much-anticipated Storytelling Festival, featuring renowned storytellers from across the nation. During the multiple-day festival there are workshops for adults and kids, as well as related ongoing events.

Our new office space in town contains an extensive bookstore and is a haven for writers who want to work away from home or conduct a workshop, a special reading, or a book launch reception.

No community program can exist without supporting that community's youth. SOMOS proudly runs a Youth Mentorship Program in which experienced adult writers are paired with junior high and high school students on a one-to-one basis. Since the program began over a decade ago, we have seen many of Taos's talented young people move on to higher learning and emerge as published writers and poets.

Nearly two decades ago, a handful of SOMOS board members came up with the idea of publishing an annual chapbook to include the work of those who participated in a Writers' Series during the calendar year. That idea evolved into *Chokecherries: A SOMOS Anthology*, celebrating its nineteenth year. Now we have this first edition of *Storied Recipes*, a one-of-a-kind fundraising cookbook, from the kitchens and minds of friends of SOMOS.

There are more secrets to our longevity: the loyalty of our members; the generosity of established and emerging writers; the various funders, public and private, who believe in the organization; and the audiences who participate in workshops, buy books, attend readings and events.

Special thanks to the board of directors and executive director who work tirelessly to keep things fresh, all while maintaining our standard as "the literary heart of Taos."

We look forward to many more years of tradition, new ideas, and exciting writing as we continue to be a home for lovers of words, reading, and now, food. Whenever and wherever you open this book, I hope you will admire, encourage, and support the written word as it exists in this small mountain town.

Bon appétit, my friends.

Alan Macrae
President of the SOMOS Board

Table of Contents

Soups & Salads

Asparagus Salad

Greens 2oz
Asparagus 2.5 oz
Hard Boiled egg 1
garnish
Red pepper strips optional

Creamy Lemon Ga
Dressing

3/4 C mayo
2 TBS Lemon Juic
1/2 tsp finely chop
Dijon Vinagre

6

7

JOAN LIVINGSTON

Caldo Verde, or Kale Soup

My sister and I stared at the plates of hamburger, potatoes, and something else our grandmother set before us. Here was Avó's idea of American food. We sniffed and knew it wasn't American at all. It wouldn't taste it either. We were convinced Avó kept a jar of secret spice in her kitchen that gave the food she served an unfamiliar, exotic flavor. We loved her too much not to eat it.

Angela Ferreira, our grandmother, was sixteen when she came by ship from Madeira to the U.S. and never saw her parents again. She married a man from her village, raised three daughters and a grandson, and worked as a weaver in a mill. Avó loved Elvis, TV wrestling, and the *National Enquirer.* She lived to 92 and was healthy to the end.

Avó also made great kale soup, which, if we were lucky, she'd make for us. One large batch lasted days. The white beans and potatoes broke down so the broth got creamy. With bread it was a meal.

My mother, her daughter, made us this Portuguese staple in the '50s and '60s. I cook a version for my kids and taught my husband to make it. I think of Avó whenever we eat it.

Joan Livingston, a member of SOMOS, is the managing editor of *The Taos News*. She was selected to read her new young adult novel *The Twin Jinn* plus adult fiction at SOMOS' 2012 Summer Writers Series.

1 pound kale, washed carefully, cut in half lengthwise and chopped

2 quarts soup stock or water

6 ounces *chourico* (chorizo) pork, turkey or chicken sausage (or any spicy sausage), thickly sliced

3 large potatoes, peeled and cut in chunks

1 can white beans

1 large onion, chopped

1 large garlic clove, minced

1-2 tablespoons olive oil

Salt and pepper to taste

Cilantro, chopped

(Optional: browned stewing beef, about 1/2 pound, or a half cabbage, cut in wedges)

Sauté onion and garlic in olive oil until translucent. Add the soup stock, kale, potatoes, sausage, and the can of beans. Bring to a boil, lower, and then simmer an hour. Add salt and pepper to taste. Ladle into bowls and garnish with minced cilantro. Serve with chunks of good bread. Makes 6 to 8 servings.

CARA COTUGNO FOX

The Italian in Me

I was raised on Julia Child meals made with butter sauces, mounds of meat and serious-looking dishes of vegetables with names that made me laugh as a youngster: endive, ratatouille, escarole. So of course I wanted to make a creamy soup as a starter for an upcoming Saturday night dinner for friends. Cream of watercress came to mind. Watercress is so upper, something.

The main course would be on the grill. I planned to set the table with mismatched soup bowls and mismatched cloth napkins and place-mats. The Martha in me. It was late spring. I gave myself plenty of time to shop, prep and cook. A precious village food store was just down the street. The produce there was drop-dead gorgeous. The beets screamed from their spritzed tiers, "Aren't we the sexiest roots you've ever seen?" I'll blame it on that.

As I happily removed the leaves and stems from the watercress and rinsed them thoroughly, I noticed that my watercress was actually parsley. Italian parsley, to be exact. Bunches and bunches of it, strained and puréed to a gawdawful grassy mess, served with full knowledge and five bottles of really good pinot gris. (Be sure to buy watercress for this recipe:)

A friend of SOMOS, Cara Cotugno Fox has been writing professionally for twenty-seven years. She has a degree in Comparative Lit., a handful of honorable mentions for poetry, and a white '68 Chevy pickup that makes her heart skip a beat.

CREAM OF WATERCRESS SOUP

(from *The Silver Palate Good Times Cookbook*)

4 tablespoons unsalted butter
2 cups finely chopped yellow onions
1/2 cup minced shallots
3 cups chicken stock
1 medium potato, peeled and diced
4 bunches watercress
1 cup heavy cream
Salt and freshly ground pepper to taste
Grated nutmeg to taste
Cayenne pepper to taste

Melt butter in a large, heavy pot over low heat. Add onions and shallots and cook, covered, until tender and lightly colored, about 25 minutes. Add the chicken stock and the potato, bring to a boil, reduce the heat, and simmer, partially covered, until the potato is tender, about 20 minutes. Meanwhile, remove the leaves and stems from the watercress and rinse thoroughly. When the potato is tender, add the watercress to the pot, cover, remove from heat, and let stand for 5 minutes. Pour the soup through a strainer, reserving the liquid, and transfer the solids to a food processor. Add 1 cup of the cooking stock and process until smooth. Return the purée to the pot, stir in heavy cream, and add 1/2 to 1 cup more stock until soup is of the desired consistency. Set over medium heat, season with salt, pepper, nutmeg, and cayenne and simmer until just heated through. Makes 4 servings.

MARIA GRAZIA SELZER

Aromas of the Past: Mom's Minestrone

I was born in Tresche-Conca, Italia. Some of the fondest memories of my early childhood in Italy are of food, and one of my favorites is a simple minestrone soup my mom made in my youth—and still makes for me, our family and dear friends.

Minestrone loosely translates to "soup made from whatever you happen to have in the house." The aroma of this wonderful dish evokes feelings of love, nurturing, comfort, and childhood innocence. Although the ingredients are simple, the end result is a delicious, full-bodied, filling meal, especially when paired with homemade, steamy-hot bread.

Maria Grazia Selzer and her husband Peter have recently moved to Taos and are looking forward to attending SOMOS events. Maria calls herself "a strong advocate of the 'slow food' movement" that started in Italy.

MINESTRONE SOUP

1 gallon (4 quarts) cold water

1 cup fresh Italian minestrone beans (such as "tongue of fire")

4 stalks celery, finely chopped

3 carrots, peeled and finely chopped

1/2 large sweet onion (Vidalia or Walla Walla), finely chopped

3 large Idaho potatoes, peeled and quartered

1 pint jar of home-canned tomatoes, or 3-4 fresh tomatoes peeled and quartered

1-1/2 cups sautéed zucchini

1-1/2 cups butternut squash, peeled and finely chopped

1-1/2 cups green cabbage, shredded and finely chopped

2 bouillon cubes or equivalent (beef preferred)

Salt and pepper to taste

1 stick butter

1/4 cup olive oil

1 to 1-1/2 cups small-size pasta

Excluding pasta, place all of the above ingredients in a large pot and bring to a light boil. Immediately reduce heat, cover, and simmer for 2 to 2-1/2 hours, stirring occasionally. Approximately 15 minutes prior to serving, using a slotted spoon, lift up any large pieces of potato, mash them with a fork and stir back into the soup. At this time add your favorite small pasta. Continue to simmer for additional 15 minutes. Makes 8 to 10 servings.

(Maria's note: If you are the type who requires precise measurements, a glass or two of good Cabernet Sauvignon during preparation will help you cope.)

GAIL GOLDEN

Comfort Food Redefined

I was raised on the bland, muscular food of mid-twentieth century America. During those years of bleak forage, I moved to New Mexico and discovered the chile pepper. Hatch, habañero, serrano, bird's eye: I eagerly learned to use them all. Now I prepare food with some sort of chile pepper several times a week. This soup recipe, adapted from *Sundays at Moosewood*, uses some of my favorite fresh vegetables and the intriguing spices of Indonesian cooking. I serve it with steamed rice or rice noodles.

Gail Golden, a jewelry artisan, has lived in Taos since 1986. As a fan of SOMOS, she has attended many SOMOS events over the years.

INDONESIAN SQUASH AND SPINACH SOUP

1 teaspoon coriander seeds

1 teaspoon ground cumin

1 teaspoon turmeric

2-5 small dried thai (bird's eye) chiles

(or chile pequin)

15 whole macadamia nuts

2-3 slices galangal

(see Gail's note below)

1 large onion

2 large garlic cloves, minced

3 tablespoon vegetable oil

2 teaspoons grated fresh ginger root

1 teaspoon salt

2 cups vegetable stock

2-3 kaffir lime leaves

(see Gail's note below)

1, 14-ounce can coconut milk

4 cups peeled and cubed butternut

or acorn squash

6 small handfuls coarsely chopped

spinach, or whole small leaves

Fresh lime juice

Grind the first five ingredients (spices, chiles and nuts) using a spice grinder or mortar and pestle. Set aside. Simmer the galangal for about 20 minutes in 1 cup water, until it is reduced to 1/2 cup. In a large soup pot, sauté the onion and garlic over medium heat until onion is translucent. Add stock, ground spice mix, kaffir lime leaves, and the 1/2 cup liquid with the galangal. Stir in coconut milk and cubed squash and simmer approximately 40 minutes until squash is tender. When ready to serve, add fresh spinach leaves and stir until just wilted. Spoon into serving bowls and squeeze fresh lime juice on top to taste. Serve with a sambal (hot relish) on the side for added heat. Makes 6 servings.

(Gail's note: I purchase galangal and kaffir lime leaves online at www.importfood.com.)

15

Reunion Salad

Fine dining? Memorable recipes? Not what I ever associated with class reunions. That is until a 1997 Michigan State mini-reunion shattered all stereotypes and added some great recipes to my personal cookbook.

From four European countries, four American teachers gathered on a February weekend in Grijzegrubben, a Dutch village with more consonants in its name than living residents. Conversation rolled through our reunion meeting place. So much to tell since we'd shared a house in southern France two years before. At that time, cooking was secondary to study. Kitchen tasks offered a rare, welcome distraction from graduate study's heavy mental work. Condensing two academic years into three summer sessions, MSU's program never gave us enough time to savor the Riviera's glorious cheeses, wines, and summer-fresh produce.

On this reunion weekend in Holland, however, we four made up for all that we'd missed in '95. Travel adventures sandwiched between slices of local Gouda. Classroom anecdotes seasoned with Chicken Marbella's Mediterranean flavors. Echoes of barely tasted French semesters burst from the freshness of this pear-gorgonzola salad.

Jean Admire, international educator and librarian, has eaten and cooked her way across five continents, creating recipes that bring "home" into the kitchen wherever she lives. SOMOS events inspire her and account for many additions to her library collection.

PEAR AND GORGONZOLA SALAD

2 ripe pears, sliced and tossed in a bit of fresh lemon juice to keep from discoloring
4 ounces gorgonzola (or Cambozola , Maytag Blue, or Roquefort) cheese, crumbled
1 head frisee lettuce (or a mix of frisee and mesclun), washed, spun dry, and torn
into bite-size pieces.
1/4 cup mayonnaise (best quality)
1/4 cup plain (unflavored) yogurt
2 tablespoons thin honey
1/4 cup walnuts, toasted and chopped (optional)

Place torn lettuce in mixing bowl. In another bowl, mix the mayonnaise and yogurt until smooth; add the honey until the dressing is suitable for pouring. Dress lettuce lightly, then arrange about a cup of greens on each salad plate. Top each plate of greens with 4 to 5 slices of pear and 1/4th of the crumbled cheese. Drizzle a bit more dressing over the top. Delicious as it is, but even better if garnished with toasted walnut pieces. Makes 4 servings.

MYA COURSEY

Mom's Macaroni-Baked Bean Salad

Couples sip cocktails, gossip, discuss the Presidential race and Communists. The men wear sports coats but no ties; the women, high heeled pumps and shirtwaists. Several smoke. Post-war jazz plays in the background. If anyone doesn't "like Ike" or prefers Fats Domino, they don't say. Welcome to Saturday evening supper club in Dallas, Texas, summer 1952.

Dinner is announced and the men happily crowd to the front of the buffet line. They bring good appetites when the Courseys host. Well-prepared and well-presented, Laura Coursey's cooking isn't fancy, but it encourages second helpings.

My mother Laura was the youngest of ten, born to Swedish immigrants in rural Wisconsin, and she learned to cook during the Depression. She married in Alaska, and in the summer of 1946 my parents moved to Dallas, where Mother embraced the culture and cuisine of her new state. Favorite recipes transformed humble ingredients into attractive, nourishing meals for family, impromptu dinner guests, and monthly gatherings of the supper club.

In winter we all loved "Yankee Chili," topped with shredded cheddar and served with cornbread. In summer we relished this pasta salad, which my mother noted on a battered recipe card as "a modern Hoppin' John."

Mya Coursey is a SOMOS fan who never makes a recipe the same way twice but kitchen tested this one exactly as shown. Find her bibliography *Storytellers: Women Writing Taos 1912-2012* at www.taos.org/women.

2 cups cooked elbow macaroni (= 1 cup dry)

1 cup vegetarian baked beans, rinsed and drained

1 bunch green onions (aka scallions), thinly sliced (white part only)

1 bunch small radishes, thinly sliced

2 tablespoons sweet pickle relish

1/2 teaspoon dry mustard (or more, to taste)

1/3 cup mayonnaise

Salt and freshly ground pepper to taste

Gently and thoroughly mix all ingredients together. Refrigerate until cool. Garnish with slices of hard-boiled egg, if desired. Keeps several days in refrigerator. Makes 6 servings as a side dish, 3 as vegetarian entrée.

SW Favorites

3 zanahorias grandes
1 taza de aceite
3 huevos

3 tazas de harina
2 tazas de azúcar
1 cucharada hoja de
— o —

3 big carrots
1 cup of oil
3 eggs

3 cups
2 1
1 soup

Add wet m
± 1/2 hour
Big dish

21

KRISTA GAYLE STEEN

Mimi's Cream of Green Chile Soup

It was around 4 a.m. in Nacogdoches, Texas, and I couldn't stand it any longer. I picked up the phone and called my sister Karla in El Paso. I knew she would be annoyed that I was calling so early, but I was desperate. The phone rang eleven times before she answered. When I told her why I was calling, she was silent for so long I thought she had fallen back to sleep.

"Let me get this straight," she said finally, sounding fully awake, "you want me to get in my car and drive halfway across the state of Texas just to meet you with a pot of Mimi's cream of green chile soup? Are you kidding?"

"No," I sighed. "I've been here for nearly six months and I haven't had any decent Mexican food. I need some green chile! I need Mimi's soup!"

"I understand," Karla said, "but sorry, Sis, no can do." And with that, she hung up the phone, and I found myself facing the bleary prospect of another trip to the local Taco Bell. All for the love of chile.

Krista Gayle Steen is a native New Mexican with a lifelong love and appreciation for the food traditions of the state. She has lived in Taos for nearly sixteen years, during which time she has attended countless SOMOS activities.

CREAM OF GREEN CHILE SOUP

1/2 pound onions, finely chopped
1/4 cup clarified butter
1/2 pound fresh green chiles, roasted, peeled, deveined and chopped
2 cups chicken stock
1 teaspoon salt
1/2 teaspoon white pepper
1 pint sour cream
1-1/2 pints heavy cream

Sauté onion in clarified butter until translucent. Add chiles and chicken stock and cook over medium heat for 25 minutes. Add salt and pepper and remove from heat. Add creams slowly, stirring constantly. Refrigerate immediately. Reheat desired amount slowly. Do not boil. Makes 2 quarts of soup.

(Krista's note: Mimi was my beloved grandmother, Mary Steen, who lived in El Paso. She always made this soup the night before, to enhance the flavor of the chiles.)

GENE GRAY

World's Greatest Chicken Tortilla Soup

My wife and I *love* tortilla soup and have been taste-testing it since we moved to Taos eleven years ago. We didn't consider making it ourselves even though we do like to cook. We thought it took in-born special talents. Our searches had centered on restaurants, upscale and down, mostly in Albuquerque, Santa Fe, and, yes, Taos. We had some pretty terrific versions and some sorry disappointments.

Then one day I found a recipe in *Penzy's Magazine* that looked promising and easy enough. So I made it a couple of times, making minor adjustments along the way. Now I happily (and humbly) share my very own recipe for "the world's greatest chicken tortilla soup."

Since retiring from real estate operations in 1994, Gene Gray has been increasingly adventurous in the kitchen. He says he and his wife Sara enjoy SOMOS programs very much.

24

CHICKEN TORTILLA SOUP

8 ounces boneless skinless chicken breasts

2, 5-ounce cans of diced tomatoes with green chiles

2, 15-ounce cans Hatch green chile enchilada sauce

2, 15-ounce cans black beans, drained and rinsed

2 cups frozen whole kernel corn

1 onion, chopped

2-3 cloves garlic, minced

4 cups (1 quart, or 32 ounces) low sodium chicken broth

1-1/2 teaspoons ground cumin

2 teaspoons Mexican (dried) oregano

1-2 teaspoons New Mexico chile powder (or to taste)

Garnishes: limes, sour cream or yogurt, avocado, Monterrey Jack, tortillas

Put all of the soup ingredients into a heavy soup kettle and cook on low heat for 2 to 3 hours. Remove chicken and shred it with two forks. Return to pot. Add the juice of 1 to 2 fresh limes and serve with additional lime wedges and sour cream or yogurt, chopped avocado, shredded Monterrey Jack cheese. Top with oven-toasted corn tortilla strips. Makes 8 to 10 servings.

(Gene's note: I usually double or triple the recipe and freeze any leftovers for a nice fast future meal. Or I just invite a crowd and we eat it all up.)

ANITA RODRIGUEZ

Quelite Soup

Quelites, known as lamb's quarters or "wild spinach" in English, grow almost everywhere in and near agricultural areas in the Southwest. They have an oak-shaped leaf with a silvery underside and a red strip on the stem. They are a staple wild food in the traditional New Mexican diet and in my family were called "Mexican vitamins," attributed with magical powers akin to Popeye's spinach. They are, in fact, extremely rich in minerals and vitamins, pesticide- and preservative-free, and outside the cash economy.

Quelites are in season in early June, and along with green chile, the hard-core Chicano freezer must be stocked with them to insure a sane and healthy winter. When you pick them, avoid the woodiest stems to save time in the kitchen; wash thoroughly in soap and a teaspoon of disinfectant, put them in a colander, pour boiling water over them, and then freeze.

Usually they are fried lightly with bacon, but I invented this soup recipe to compliment open-faced vegetarian sandwiches made with homemade herb buns with tomato sauce and grated cheese on top.

Anita Rodriguez was born and raised in Taos and comes from ten generations of quelite-eating ancestors. She is a painter, writer, cook, Tarot-card reader, and a friend of SOMOS.

4 strips bacon (optional)

1-1/2 tablespoons olive oil (or bacon grease)

1/2 onion, diced

2 cloves garlic, minced

3 cups cleaned quelites

1/2 cup chicken stock

2 cups half-and-half

1 teaspoon dried marjoram

Salt to taste

Chile pequin to taste

If using bacon, fry until crisp and set aside. If not, heat olive oil in a large frying pan, add onion and garlic, brown lightly and then add quelites and chicken stock. Cook quelites just until limp; do not overcook. Then put into a blender, with half-and-half, marjoram, and salt to taste. Blend until smooth. Serve hot with chile pequin on the side and crumbled bacon sprinkled on top. Makes 4 servings.

Chile Rellenos, Muy Bien

My wife Melissa grows some of the best green chile in all of Taos County. My opinion is that everything she grows is darn good — and I'm not alone in thinking this.

Recently *The Taos News* did a story in their "Home & Garden" section featuring Melissa and the Taos County Women Farmers Group. She is one of its founding members. This group, which now numbers more than thirty, includes women with home gardens, as well as those who run commercial farms. There are beekeepers, goat herders, community-supported agriculture farmers, and women who sell to restaurants and at farmers' markets. As reporter Ariana Kramer quoted Melissa in the article, "Good food is really important to me, and local food is best."

My wife grows chiles (among many other things), which, when roasted and peeled, turn into delicious dishes that are *muy bien*. Here is her recipe for chile rellenos. It takes ninety days to make, but it's well worth the wait.

A thirty-year resident of Taos, Ed Bell is the secretary of the Acequia Madre del Canon del Norte. He describes himself as "housebroken" and a lover of green chile "in all its iterations." He and Melissa enjoy attending SOMOS events.

6 fresh green chiles (preferably home-grown), roasted and peeled
6 slices of Monterey Jack cheese
Flour for dredging
2 eggs, separated
2 tablespoons flour
Pinch of salt
Oil for frying
Fresh flour tortillas (preferably homemade)
Guacamole
Sour Cream

Cut cheese into slices to fit the chiles and stuff them. Roll each in flour. Beat egg whites until stiff but not dry, then fold in yolks that have been lightly beaten. Sift 2 tablespoons flour and salt over the eggs and fold in carefully. Scoop mixture onto a plate and place chiles on top, turning to completely coat them with the batter. Pour about an inch of oil in a frying pan and heat. Slip the chiles one by one onto a saucer with as much batter as possible, then push with a spoon into the oil. When golden on the underside, flip over and cook until golden all over, about 30 seconds a side. Remove with a slotted spoon and drain on paper towels. Spread guacamole and sour cream on a homemade flour tortilla, lay one chile relleno inside, and roll up, burrito-style. Makes 4 to 6 servings.

DAN CASSIDY

The Tyranny of the Potluck

Anyone who is a parent or part of an organization, or who works with more than two people, will inevitably take part in the ritual of the potluck. As simple as this may sound, it is in fact a complex and devious test inflicted upon newcomers in order to place them in the social strata.

Potluck participants tend to take one of the following strategies: gourmet (Duck à l'Orange, eg), overachievement (individual homemade mini-quiches with home-cured bacon), traditional (tuna-noodle casserole) and the en route purchase (pizza), a subset of which is the anonymous offering of chips and salsa. I have at one time or another attempted each of these tactics.

Embracing the Taos Potluck Lifestyle, I felt I needed to come up with a dish that would go beyond the usual salty, sweet and quick fare—make something, perhaps, even for the vegetarian contingency. An early incarnation, vegetable stew with corn bread on the side, eventually evolved into this dish, a vegetarian New Mexican alternative to the shepherd's pie of my youth.

When Dan Cassidy moved from the U.K. to New Jersey in 1991, he could not find an Indian restaurant to satiate his curry cravings, so he had to learn to cook for himself. Many years and a culinary degree later, he relocated to Taos. He attends as many SOMOS readings as his schedule allows.

GREEN CHILE TAMALE PIE

For the pie filling:

2 cups chopped onions

2 cloves garlic, minced

1/2 teaspoon salt

1/2 cup chopped, roasted green Hatch chiles

1 tablespoon vegetable oil

2 teaspoons ground cumin

2 cups cubed potatoes

3 cups peeled, cubed sweet potatoes

1 tablespoon lime juice

For the topping:

1 cup cornmeal

2 tablespoons all-purpose flour

1-1/2 teaspoons baking powder

1/2 teaspoon baking soda

1/2 teaspoon salt

1/2 cup corn kernels (fresh or frozen)

2 eggs, beaten

1/2 cup buttermilk

2 tablespoons vegetable oil

Preheat oven to 350 degrees. Make the filling: Sauté the onions, garlic and salt in the oil in a Dutch oven or ovenproof skillet. Once the onions are tender, add the green chiles and cumin and cook about 5 minutes. Add the potatoes, sweet potatoes and 2 cups water. Bring to a boil. Reduce heat and simmer until the potatoes are tender, about 20 minutes. Stir in lime juice.

Make the topping:

Combine the dry ingredients, plus the corn, in a large bowl. In a separate bowl, whisk together the wet ingredients and add them to the dry ingredients, gently folding to incorporate. Spread topping mixture over the vegetables to cover evenly. Bake for about 30 minutes. Makes about 4 servings.

ANNETTE ARELLANO

Grandma Brito's Sopapillas

My Grandma Brito and her calico cat Bootsie lived alone, but my siblings and I would visit all the time when we were young. It was the place to be when we were hungry, tired, or needed a story to listen to. Grandma Brito would cook some of my favorite dishes, including sopapillas.

I loved to watch her at the wood stove deep frying the sopapillas and serving them warm and fresh to eat with our beans, potatoes, and chiles. She would let the dough rise on the kitchen table while she heated up the stove and the oil in a large cast iron skillet.

Before she began the procedure, though, Bootsie would jump on her lap and hope for a taste of something from Grandma's hand. Grandma always had a treat for Bootsie, and the cat was accustomed to eating at the table from Grandma's lap.

One day, when Grandma was cleaning up the table and putting the scraps in her hand, my little brother came out from behind the stove with the cat's dish and asked if he could have more. Grandma was a bit upset that he had eaten all of Bootsie's food. We all laughed and wondered maybe that was why Bootsie liked Grandma's lap and hand-fed scraps instead of leftovers in a dark corner behind the stove, along with a little boy who was hungry enough to eat it all himself.

That little brother is now grown up and raises many different kinds of domestic and farm animals. He still eats seconds most of the time, especially when one of us makes sopapillas.

Annette Arellano is a local Taoseña who has many kitchen memories and childhood dreams that have come true. She is a former UNM-Taos student, a friend of SOMOS, and a short-story writer.

SOPAPILLAS

3 cups warm water
1 package dry yeast
1 tablespoon sugar
6 cups all-purpose flour
2 tablespoons lard or fat
1 heaping tablespoon salt
3-4 cups cooking oil (depending on size of skillet) for deep frying

In a large mixing bowl, mix the ingredients for the "sponge" (warm water, yeast, and sugar) and let stand from 15 to 60 minutes. Then add the dry ingredients to the sponge and knead by hand for 10 minutes. Add more flour or warm water (gradually, if needed) to make a soft dough that is not too sticky nor too stiff. Separate dough into rolls about 3/4-cup in size and then roll each one out like a tortilla, flat and thin. Cut into wedges, if desired. Fry in hot oil in skillet at a high temperature. When both sides are crispy and brown, remove from skillet, drain, cool and eat. Makes about 3 dozen.

Meaty Matters

Bacon & Egg Tart.

½ lb. Bacon.
2 Eggs.
1 cup of Milk.
Cayenne Pepper.
4 Tbs. Self Raising Flo
½ cup Cheddar Cheese

Mix all the ingre. tog
greased dish. Put a litt
on top. Bake at 350°
Could also add

35

Elk Chile

Get up at four in the morning. Remember where you are. On top of a mountain. Struggle out of your sleeping bag, dress, pee, find your rifle. Flashlight in hand, stagger off into the wilderness. Remember your way. Find the spot you decided on yesterday and sit until the sun comes up in increments, giving you a tiny insight into how the world works. Hope that the squirrels and ravens don't spot you before you get a good shot.

A heart or neck shot is best. Calm your racing heart. Squeeze. Follow the great beast into the forest until it dies. Sit by it until its last breath. Thank your beast for its life. Dress it out and carry the meat home. Hang it in a cool dry place for ten days to two weeks. Butcher and freeze all but one roast, to be used for this chile stew.

Alan Macrae has lived in Taos for many years, first in a log cabin in Carson, then in a series of old and new houses in the town of Taos. He is a writer, fisherman, occasional hunter, builder, and the president of the board of SOMOS.

2 pound elk roast
2 tablespoons oil
2 tablespoons all-purpose flour
2-4 tablespoons finely ground red chile (see procedure below)
Salt to taste

Cook the roast for 4 to 6 hours at 225 degrees in a dutch oven. When cool, cut into bite-size pieces. Sauté these pieces in oil, adding flour then water to make a roux; then mix in roasted red chile. Simmer the elk in the sauce for 15-20 minutes, for the flavors to marry.

To make the red chile:
Take a ristra and strip a handful of chiles that have dried in the fall sun until they are a deep, dark red. Roast them, break them up and sift them until they are the consistency of ground coffee. The amount of chile you add to the roux determines the piquancy of the chile. Be generous. Chile is good for you. Salt to taste.

ANDREA MEYER

Stuffed Roast Leg of Goat

It isn't every day that you're obliged to harvest your meat for the evening meal. Such was the situation I found myself in at the onset of my food career. I had long cherished the handmade goat cheeses of Quillisascut Farm on the northeast border of Washington State. So when I heard of their newest venture, "Quillisascut School of Domestic Arts," I applied as a culinary student and was somehow accepted.

I arrived at a picturesque, fully sustainable farm flanked by the Huckleberry Mountains, peach and apple orchards, flocks of wild turkeys, vegetable gardens, milking parlors, grape orchards, and lamb and goat herds. After four days of 4 a.m. wake-ups, incredible family-style meals (made exclusively from farm and foraged ingredients), tending crops, making cheese and learning to milk the beloved goats, it was my turn to make dinner. As it happened, it was also the day we would learn to butcher a goat.

In the course of the day, my food and eating consciousness was profoundly altered. I was responsible for preparing a meal that would appropriately honor this creature, who only yesterday we were calling by name, petting, milking, and sending back out into the pasture to graze and live in leisure. This was a responsibility like no other I'd ever encountered.

Finally, determining that perhaps the knowledge of my Russian ancestry would support me, spiritually at least, I decided on a Georgian-style cilantro-walnut stuffed leg of goat. Thankfully, and very gratefully, it was delicious.

Andrea Meyer is a local food devotee and improvisational cook who loves to create on the fly. She is currently the chef at The Love Apple, manager of the Taos Farmers Market, and a friend and fan of SOMOS. For more, go to: foodfromfarms@gmail.com.

For the stuffing:

2 cups pecans

1 tablespoon garlic

1 cup fresh cilantro

1 tablespoon ground coriander

1/2 cup crumbled feta cheese

Juice and zest of one lemon

1/2 cup olive oil

Salt to taste

Puree all of the above in a food processor
or blender and set aside.

For the meat:

1 butterflied leg of goat
(about 4 pounds), at room temperature

2 tablespoons chopped garlic

1 teaspoon salt

1 teaspoon black pepper

To prepare the meat:

Spread the leg out, skin side down, and rub it with the chopped garlic, salt and pepper. (Ideally, allow the rubbed meat to sit at room temperature for about an hour before cooking.) Preheat oven to 375 degrees. Spread the stuffing/puree across the boned surface of the meat. Roll the meat (from the long side) to enclose the stuffing. Tie the leg every 2-3 inches with kitchen twine to hold it all together. Rub the outer surface with olive oil and sprinkle with salt and pepper. Place in a roasting pan and roast for about 1-1/4 hours (to an internal temperature of 130 degrees). Allow to rest about 15 minutes before carving. Makes 8 to 10 servings.

(Andrea's note: This recipe is a simplified version of the one I made that day, incorporating ingredients that we have available here in the Southwest. Lamb may be substituted for goat.)

LARA SANTORO

Coda alla Vaccinara, or Oxtail Stew

When the restaurant Da Checchino opened its doors in the late 1800s, it was to provide wine, olives and cheese to the construction crew at work on Rome's largest slaughterhouse.

Years later, when it was the slaughterhouse's turn to open its doors for business, the owners of the restaurant found themselves confronted at the end of every working day by starving apprentices whose butchering skills were confined to flaying and halving and whose pay often consisted of the *quinto quarto*: the head, entrails, shins and tail of the animal. Basically, the parts nobody else would eat.

More out of pity than culinary curiosity, the restaurant learned how to soften the cartilage in tails, distend the fibrous lining in stomachs, and impart real flavor to gelatinous brains. Out of this unlikely pairing came celebrated Roman dishes like *coda alla vaccinara* and *rigatoni alla pagata*. But it gets better.

During the 1980s, when Italy was awash with money and Rome was the capital of every unholy alliance ever made over a meal, you couldn't get a table at Da Checchino's if you tried.

Lara Santoro's new novel, *The Boy*, is scheduled to be published by Little, Brown in January 2013. She is the author of another work of fiction, *Mercy*. She is also a big fan of SOMOS.

1 cow's tail (sold as oxtail here), cut into bits

Lard (do not use butter or olive oil)

Pig fat (whatever you can scrape together from bacon or pancetta fat)

Parsley

1 onion, 1 carrot, 1 celery stalk—each cut into dice

1 garlic clove

1 glass of white wine

3-4 tablespoons of good tomato sauce

Salt and freshly ground pepper

Throw the tail pieces into boiling water. Once the water comes to a boil again, remove and lay aside. Sauté onion and carrot in lard and pig fat until soft, then add tail bits and turn until brown. Add salt and pepper to taste. Splash repeatedly with white wine (do not add all at once), until fully evaporated. Add tomato sauce diluted in about a quart of warm water. Cover and cook over a very low flame for 4 hours. Add the diced celery, cover, and simmer for another 30 minutes. Serve piping hot in a bowl with its juices. Makes 8 servings.

(Lara's note: This is my own version of *coda alla vaccinara*. I've never made it in a crockpot, but it might work, if left to cook slowly overnight.)

Kidney Stew

One day in August 1997, Youssef arrived at the front door of my house in Lastoursville, Gabon, at noon with a surprise — a bag of fresh beef kidneys from the town's only butcher. "*Rognons!*" he announced with a big grin, "*pour un ragoût!*"

Kidney stew? I hadn't had kidney stew, I realized, since I was a child. How did Youssef know I loved kidney stew? Here was a man who understood me.

As a child I'd loved all of my mother's cooking, especially what she could do with meat. Her whole roast chickens were golden, moist, and tender. Her beef braises and stews were richly flavored and melted in my mouth. But, oddly enough, what I loved most was her kidney stew, with its softly rounded chunks of meat that tasted actually sweet to me.

"How many kids in this world like kidney stew?" my father bellowed from the head of the table. "You are a *carnivorous* animal," he said to me with a wink.

That August afternoon in my kitchen in Lastoursville, Youssef and I prepared our kidney stew together, the first of many meals we would cook and eat together. Our kidney stew was sweet and delicious. Just like my mother's.

Bonnie Lee Black, an instructor in both the English and Culinary Arts departments at UNM-Taos, read from her award-winning memoir-with-recipes, *How to Cook a Crocodile*, at SOMOS' Winter Writers' Series 2011. This recipe is from that book. For more, go to www.bonnieleeblack.com

1 pound beef kidneys

1 teaspoon salt

1 medium onion, chopped

1 large clove garlic, minced

4 tablespoons unsalted butter

Flour (for dredging)

1/3 cup dry red wine

2 tablespoon tomato paste

2 cups (1 can) beef broth, or 1 beef bouillon cube,

plus 2 cups water

Salt and freshly ground pepper to taste

Wash kidneys, trim away any fat, membrane, or connective tissue, and place in a bowl. Add 1 teaspoon salt, and water to cover; allow to soak for at least 30 minutes. Drain, rinse, and pat dry; cut into bite-size chunks. Sauté chopped onion and minced garlic in butter over medium heat until softened. Dredge kidney pieces in flour and cook with onions and garlic until slightly browned. Add wine, tomato paste, and beef broth (or bouillon plus water) and bring to a boil. Lower heat, cover pan, and cook gently for about 10 minutes. Season to taste with salt and freshly ground black pepper. Serve over steamed white rice. Makes 4 servings.

Birds without Bones

In the late 1950s, the Cornell University Experiment Station in Geneva, New York, attracted brilliant researchers from all over the world to work on agricultural projects. Dr. David Hand headed the Experiment Station. His kindly wife Eleanor understood the loneliness of women whose husbands were busily involved in their research projects; wives were often homesick for their native lands. Eleanor devised a plan to offer them friendship and support.

She created an international cooking club. The women in this newly formed club met in each other's kitchens to make a favorite dish and then enjoy eating together afterwards. Eleanor's plan had the desired effect. It fed our hearts and our stomachs, as we became friends over delicious dishes from around the world.

One of the dishes in particular stands out in my mind. A woman from Norway guided us in fixing a meat dish, which she called "Birds without Bones." It became a favorite of mine when, as a new bride, I wanted to offer something special for dinner, a step above hamburgers.

Margery Reading, a retired psychologist and a friend of SOMOS, moved with her husband George to Taos permanently in 1995.

44

NORWEGIAN STUFFED HAMBURGERS

1-1/2 pounds ground round steak, divided

1/2 teaspoon nutmeg, divided

1-1/2 teaspoons salt, divided

1/4 teaspoon ground cloves

2 tablespoons bone marrow

Freshly ground pepper to taste

Oil for browning meat

1 cup (or more) sherry wine (not cooking sherry)

Take one-third of the ground round (1/2 pound) and chop it finely with a knife (or use a food processor). To this finely ground meat, add 1/4 teaspoon nutmeg, 1/4 teaspoon ground cloves, the bone marrow, 1 teaspoon of the salt, and pepper to taste. Combine well. Divide into 6 equal-size balls.

To the remaining (1 pound) ground meat, add 1/4 teaspoon nutmeg, 1/2 teaspoon salt, and pepper to taste. Combine well. On a moistened surface, using a 1/4-cup measure, create 6 patties. Flatten each patty, and roll the flattened meat around the filling to form a small "bird." Brown lightly in a heavy skillet; add sherry, and simmer, covered, for about 20 minutes. Serve with sautéed onions, peas, tomatoes, and the starch of your choice. Makes 4 to 6 servings.

MELISSA CONTI

Cowboy Steak

I grew up in Connecticut in the seventies with two older brothers who expected me to keep up with them. I learned how to balance my softer female side with a bold male influence. They liked cars, motorcycles, target shooting, and taught me to like them, too. My oldest brother, a Harley guy, is a professional chef; the other one, a father and business director, loves to fish and grill outdoors. Under their influence, I bought a motorcycle that fit my smaller size and learned to target shoot.

I took target-shooting lessons with a master trainer who I'd heard was at a high level in that field—a man who trains police officers. George turned out to be a handsome Italian-American with many sides to him. From the very beginning I was able to hit a bull's-eye easily and he was impressed. We talked about guns—and food. Sometime during our lessons we began exchanging recipes, and he just happened to have copies of his favorites on hand.

Committed to safety, I practiced, followed all the rules, and one day George presented me with a gun license and his recipe for Cowboy Steak. He said it was his "greatest" and it's become a favorite among the carnivores in my life.

Melissa Conti is the owner and operator of Seaport Salon in Norwalk, Connecticut, and is a mother, grandmother, beach walker, cook, and lover of adventure on wheels. She writes in her journals and goes to SOMOS readings during summer visits to Taos.

4 bone-in or boneless rib eye steaks 1-1/4 inch thick

1 tablespoon coffee beans (light roast) Costa Rican (or similar)

1 tablespoon peppercorns

1/8 teaspoon paprika

1/2 tablespoon garlic powder

1/2 tablespoon sea salt

1 tablespoon Old Bay seasoning

Grind all of the dry ingredients in a coffee grinder under max cup setting and fine grind. Rub steaks with mixture and let sit to reach room temperature. Grill on high to medium-high heat. Serve with a green salad and a hearty red wine. Makes 4 servings.

Beef Tenderloin with Spicy Dressing

I have always loved to cook, so it came as no surprise to my husband when I entered the 1993 New Mexico Beef Cook-Off. I created this recipe using beef tenderloin. But because beef tenderloin is pricy, I never actually cooked the dish before I submitted the recipe.

Then, lo and behold, I got a call saying I was one of the five finalists in the state. The next thing I knew I was ordering a beef tenderloin, collecting the rest of the ingredients, packing pots, pans and a serving dish, and driving to the university in Los Cruces for the contest. There was a giant room with five cooking stations. When the rules were explained, my heart palpitated. We had exactly one hour to prepare the dish, and present it on a serving platter for the judges.

Since I had never actually cooked it, I had no idea how long it would take me. All of a sudden I heard, "One minute!" At that point everyone had to throw in his or her apron. Miracles do happen. I finished in time and won third place.

Nancy Enderby and her husband own Horse Feathers located on Kit Carson Road in Taos and sell cowboy collectibles, boots and hats (www.cowboythings.com). She thinks SOMOS is "terrific."

2 onions, peeled and quartered

1 tablespoon olive oil

1 clove garlic, crushed

1, 12-ounce jar roasted red peppers, cut into 1/4-inch strips

2 pounds beef tenderloin, center cut

2-inch piece fresh ginger, peeled and finely grated

2 tablespoons packed brown sugar

3 cloves garlic, crushed

4 jalapeño peppers, seeded and finely minced

1/2 cup olive oil

4 tablespoons lime juice

1 cup fresh cilantro, chopped

1 teaspoon pepper seasoning salt

Sauté onion in 1 tablespoon olive oil and garlic until soft. Add red pepper strips and keep warm. Place beef tenderloin on a roasting pan. Roast at 425 degrees for 30-40 minutes for rare or until desired doneness. In a jar with a tight-fitting lid, mix remaining ingredients. Shake until well blended. In a small saucepan, heat dressing for 5 minutes. To serve, slice beef thinly and place on a serving platter. Garnish with peppers and onions. Drizzle with half of the dressing. Serve remaining dressing on the side. Makes 8 servings.

NORM FERGUSON

Christmas Beef Tenderloin

In 1958 I was fourteen and living in suburban Philadelphia. Christmas was coming up and that meant dinner at Aunt Mary's.

It was the same fare each year—string beans, mashed potatoes, gravy, stuffed mushrooms, incredible rolls and more. The centerpiece of the meal was a large roast beef tenderloin. But there was a problem: Uncle Henry liked his meat well done, so the roast came out resembling a charcoal briquette. It was dry and tasteless, but no one had the courage to tell Aunt Mary.

I couldn't stand another Christmas eating cremated beef. So that day I brought along a piece of "modern technology" I hoped would save the dinner—a meat thermometer. In the kitchen I saw a gorgeous hunk of meat awaiting ruination. I showed Aunt Mary the meat thermometer, and she said she'd never seen one before, which seemed obvious to me. I told her the ends could be well done and the center could be a little red for those who might prefer that. She agreed. I spent my first minutes being a chef.

A skeptical crowd waited in the dining room. When red juice flowed from the first cut, I saw broad smiles around the table — all thanks to fourteen-year-old me and modern technology.

Norm Ferguson, a friend of SOMOS, is a retired college professor who has lived in Taos for twelve years.

4-to 5-pound trimmed whole beef tenderloin

Coarse kosher salt

2 tablespoons extra-virgin olive oil

2 tablespoons black peppercorns, coarsely cracked in mortar with pestle

Sprinkle entire surface of beef tenderloin with coarse kosher salt. Place beef on rack set over large rimmed baking sheet. Refrigerate uncovered at least 24 hours or up to 36 hours. Let beef stand at room temperature 1 hour before roasting. Position rack in center of oven and preheat to 425 degrees. Rub beef all over with oil; sprinkle with 2 tablespoons cracked peppercorns, pressing to adhere. Return beef to rack on baking sheet and roast until instant-read thermometer ("modern technology") inserted into thickest part of meat registers 125°F for medium-rare (135°F to 140°F in thinnest part), about 30 minutes. Remove roast from oven and let rest 15 minutes. Cut roast crosswise into 1/2-inch-thick slices; arrange on platter. Makes 10 servings.

MIRIAM FEDER

Baby Back Ribs

At the age of forty-six I had my first Jewish boyfriend. Baby back ribs were his favorite. My thinking went like this: ribs-are-food-is-love. I talked the whole process through with the butcher at the designer grocery store. I took copious notes: precooking, stripping away the membrane, grilling, doneness, sauce. I opened up the package at home, panicked and called the butcher again, taking down a slightly different version.

My little Kosher-girl hands were fearful: wash; wash again. Could this possibly be worth it?

Yes. The results were outstanding, delicious, seductive and appreciated. They became my event barbeque food. Everyone, I discovered, loves baby back ribs—vegetarians, low-fatters, and especially my Jewish friends.

In time, I grew less fearful and finally comfortable enough to return to my usual slapdash ways. "They've been in there how long?" "I forgot to pre-cook them." "I'm not messing with that membrane-thing." "I could have sworn I had sauce. I'll just mix all these ends-of-jars together." Every batch was different, every batch delicious. I learned there are no secrets; anything works.

Miriam Feder is a playwright, essayist, performer, and producer working in Portland, Oregon. She has performed in Taos and fell in love with SOMOS (2008). Find her at http://miriamfeder.com.

Here is my "recipe": I use an old-fashioned charcoal Weber kettle and I figure 1/2 a rack per person, serving more women than men. Choose 2 to 3 of these flavors: spicy, fruity, sour, garlicky, or smoky. You have a flavoring opportunity at the beginning—I suggest a rub with plenty of salt, pepper and garlic. Then you have a sauce opportunity later on. I like fruity with a little acid and heat.

Preheat the oven to about 200 degrees. Loosen the membrane on the bone side of the rack with a table knife and try to peel it off in one movement. Put the rub on the ribs, put the ribs in a pan deep enough to catch the fat runoff and roast the ribs slowly for at least 1-1/2 hours. Allow for about an hour on the grill. There can be time between the cooking rounds. Use direct or indirect heat on the grill. Use the last 10 minutes on the grill to brush on thin layers of sauce, turn, watch, baste, turn, etc. Most sauces have sugar and will burn if you leave the ribs unattended. Remove after the hour, let them rest just a little and serve. They go with everything.

J. FRANCESCA GRANO

Close Range Sausage and Peppers

Back in the sixties, while working for a doctor in a rough section of Waterbury, Connecticut, we had a patient who had "accidentally" shot himself. Twice. In the leg. Not wishing to go to an emergency room and answer questions, he came to our office. Dr. Rocco and I treated him and quietly sent him home.

A few days later, driving home from work, I noticed I was being followed. The passenger in the car was our infamous gunshot patient. I was instantly nervous and tried to speed through a yellow light. I didn't make it. It turned red.

I watched as he got out of the car and limped toward me with something in his hand. He tapped my car window. He was smiling and holding a covered plate. Trembling, I rolled down the window and heard him say, "Thank you."

Knowing that food is the best thank you for Italians, I accepted his gift of sausages and peppers. He also gave me a small gold horn charm, "to ward off evil spirits," he said. I always share this recipe. But I'm keeping the charm.

Francesca Grano, who is retired from a long and colorful career in health care, is a writer, poet, and volunteer coordinator for SOMOS' writers series.

ITALIAN SAUSAGE AND PEPPERS

2 tablespoons olive oil

1-2 red or sweet onions, sliced

3 bell peppers – red, yellow, and orange – sliced

1-3 packages Italian sausages (hot or mild, as you wish)

1 cup shredded mild cheese, such as mozzarella

Grease a baking dish (approximately 9 x 14-inch) with olive oil. Place a layer of onions on the bottom. Cut the sausages into 1-inch slices and place on top of onions. Place sliced peppers on top of sausages. Repeat until all is used. Bake, covered, at 350 degrees about one hour. Sprinkle with cheese, and return to oven to cook about 15 more minutes, uncovered. Makes 6 to 8 servings.

Chicken or Egg...

Buttermilk

2½ cups Butter or Marg (I use
3 cups Butter milk
16 cups Flour.
½ cups Sugar
⅓ tsp. Salt.

2 Pkts. Cream of Tartar. (4 teas
1" Bicarb. (± 2 teaps)

3 Eggs.

Method: Sieve dry ingredients to
butter. Mix cream of Tartar
one cup of Butter milk
this mixture.

Stir mixture into d
add. the other 2 cups
& knead well.
Bake in 350°F

Instead of Butterm
or lemon. Sm als.
little with wate

Cut into small o
for ± 6 h
oven ou outside

57

HANS VAN HEYST

German Flammkuchen, New Mexico Style

During the time I was in Germany on business, my wife and I visited an old village. A German couple came to help us with some information, in German, on what to see and how to get there. They even invited us to come to their home for a cup of coffee. We thought it was just a polite comment, but they insisted we come that afternoon. We accepted.

When we arrived they said that since it was late in the afternoon, they felt we should have a glass of wine and some *flammkuchen* instead of coffee. We said okay. That's how I learned about *flammkuchen* and how to make them. At work the next day I told my German colleagues about this. They couldn't believe it, because "Germans just don't do these things." We proved them wrong, and we ended up with a great recipe, which we've since adapted to our life in New Mexico.

Hans Van Heyst, a new friend of SOMOS, is a retired mechanical engineer who worked in developing analytical instrumentation and now likes to experiment with cooking and weaving.

2 flour tortillas

1/4 cup crème fraiche

1/4 cup finely chopped peppers

A pinch of nutmeg

1/4 cup finely chopped onions

1/4 cup finely chopped cooked chicken

(or lunch meat, or whatever cooked meat you have on hand)

Cover tortillas with about 1/8-inch thick layer of crème fraiche. Sprinkle with the cooked meat, onion and pepper. Sprinkle nutmeg to taste. Place directly on a preheated grill over medium heat. Cook until crisp, which only will take about one minute. Be careful not to overcook. (Can also be cooked in an oven on broil.) Cut like a pizza. Makes 1 lunch- or dinner-size serving or 4 servings as an appetizer, cut in quarters.

MARGARET J. HANSEN

Highland Paella

In the seventies in a Midwestern university town, I had a good friend who introduced me to American foods—not exotic foods, but prepared in a manner completely different than I had experienced. An example: the grilled chocolate sandwich. At first I was skeptical. Or perhaps I was just a food snob.

The idea became more inviting when she told her parents' story. Her mother, an eastern European distinguished brunette, was a concert pianist. Her father, a blond-haired, soft-faced Englishman, composed show tunes. My friend grew up in a house with music, rhyme and frivolity. It must have been like having Dorothy Fields and Jerome Kern (in reversed roles) for parents.

I realized that these two young parents in their musical charm had little time for cooking and possibly invented putting a chocolate bar between two slices of bread and grilling it. Or maybe they were trying to recreate the French *pain au chocolat*. Regardless, I offer this idea for the times when a celebration is a must and there is no time for paella or cheesecake. A little champagne might help.

When there is time, however, I search my 1970's edition of *Joy of Cooking* and spain-recipes.com, see what's fresh in the market, and create something like this. Serve this paella with Spanish wine, guitar music, or even show tunes.

Margaret J. Hansen retired with her partner from a twenty-five year chiropractic practice in the Midwest. In Taos she writes about those adventures and more. She contributes to SOMOS whenever possible.

3/4 cup olive oil (approximately)

1 or 2 red bell peppers, sliced in chunks

1 plump heirloom tomato, sliced in meaty wedges, without seeds

1/4 pound fresh peas, shelled

6 big shitake mushrooms, sliced

1 lemon (cut in wedges)

1-2/3 cups Arborio rice

4 cups (32 ounces) best-quality chicken broth

1 pound chicken, cut into 1-inch strips

1 chorizo sausage, sliced thin

1, 10-ounce can baby clams, rinsed (reserve liquid)

1/3 pound small frozen scallops, rinsed and dried (reserve liquid)

Thyme, rosemary, saffron, salt

Preheat oven to 350 degrees. In a saucepan, heat chicken broth and strained liquid from clams and scallops. Add saffron to taste. Sauté chicken in olive oil with rosemary, thyme and sprinkle of salt. Set aside. Sauté chorizo in olive oil, set aside. Lightly sauté shitakes. Set aside. Add olive oil to skillet, add the Arborio rice to coat and warm it. Pour in warmed saffron broth. Add peas, peppers, tomato, meats, and mushrooms with chicken at the top. Place in oven with lid on for about 30 to 40 minutes. Lightly sauté clams in olive oil with lemon juice and place in a ring around paella to steam for final five minutes. Sauté scallops in butter with thyme and lemon juice reduction. Serve paella with scallops and lemon wedge. Makes 6 to 8 servings.

KIRA ROSLER

Spanish Chicken Cutlets and Olive Rice

It's March. The baby is barely four months old, his father and I are adjusting to parenthood, and we're temporarily living with my mother in her two-bedroom apartment near Long Island Sound in Connecticut. The dining area has been converted into a nursery. The kitchen is small but has all the cooking essentials.

I need to do something else besides nursing my baby, changing diapers and sleeping. I plan a feast. Baby Dante's dad and grandma Melissa are skeptical but agree to prep and pass the baby around while I direct the show—chopping, baby-sitting, measuring, slicing. It's cold outside, but we open the door to relieve the chaos of "too many cooks in the kitchen."

Everyone has a different opinion and method. By the time we're ready to eat buffet-style (because the dining table is stored in the attic to make room for the baby-changing table), Dante is asleep. This dish turned out to be excellent and we'll make it again when he grows up.

Kira Rosler and her small family have since moved into their own digs. She attends Norwalk Community College and is studying nursing. Her grandmother has been involved in the SOMOS organization for two decades and made Kira attend readings whenever she visited Taos in summers past.

3 cups chicken stock

1-1/2 cups white rice

5 tablespoons good olive oil

4, 6-ounce boneless, skinless, chicken breasts

Salt and freshly ground black pepper

1 cup all-purpose flour

2 teaspoons paprika

2 eggs

1-1/2 cups slivered almonds

1/2 cup plain breadcrumbs

A handful of flat-leaf parsley

1, 9-ounce package frozen artichoke hearts

4 piquillo peppers or 2 roasted red peppers, chopped

1/2 cup pitted, chopped green olives

Leaves of 1 fresh thyme sprig

1/3 cup dry sherry

2 tablespoons butter, cut in small pieces

Bring stock to boil, stir in rice and 1 tablespoon olive oil. Cover, reduce heat to low, and cook about 15 minutes. Add artichokes, peppers, olives, and stir to combine. Cook 5 more minutes. Add thyme leaves and fluff with a fork. Set aside.

Preheat oven to 375 degrees. Cut through chicken breasts; butterfly them open. Season both sides with salt and pepper. Pour flour, paprika, salt, black pepper onto a dish. In a bowl, beat eggs with a splash of water. Process nuts, breadcrumbs and parsley in a food processor; pour onto plate. Coat chicken first in flour, then egg, then nut mixture. Heat 4 tablespoons olive oil over medium-high heat in large skillet; add chicken; brown on both sides, finish in oven until deeply golden and cooked through. Remove chicken to platter; add sherry to pan, and whisk in butter over low heat. Spoon sauce over chicken and serve with rice. Makes 4 servings.

Grandma Lindsey's Chicken an' Dumplin's

I was too little to help, but I watched Mimaw intently, trying to learn her kitchen magic: watching her make her addictive, thick, rich, savory chicken stew.

Unfortunately, I was usually banished from the kitchen for infractions before witnessing the process in full. For twenty years, I wrestled with producing her results from memory. Not even her *ingredients* were written down.

Over the years, I've managed to master a wrist-flour technique here, a signature taste there, but the main pillowy, succulent dumplin's eluded me. Then, about four years ago, I told my Dad my dilemma, and he said, to both my joy and embarrassment, "Self-rising flour." Of course!

So I spent the next few hours exploring this miracle flour and its purpose in Mimaw's dumplin's. At last, late in the evening ... perfection. As if I'd just been handed an Oscar, I gleefully phoned family members, screeching, "I figured it out! I figured it out!"

From childhood worship to adult mastery, here is the recipe that, until this moment, has never been written down.

Welcome Lindsey was born in northern Louisiana and moved to Taos fourteen years ago. She has a great love of all types of cuisine, but cherishes Southern cooking if only for sentimentality. She has attended and enjoyed countless SOMOS events.

For the Chicken Stock

1, 3-5-pound chicken
2 teaspoons oregano
1 onion, chopped
1 carrot, coarsely chopped
1-2 ribs celery, coarsely chopped
Salt and pepper to taste

Place all of the chicken stock ingredients in a large pot and fill with water until the chicken floats (about 6 quarts). Bring to a boil, then lower heat and simmer, covered, for about 30-45 minutes, depending on the chicken's size. Allow to cool. Remove/strain the solids from the stock and discard the vegetables. Remove skin and debone chicken. Over medium-high heat, bring the stock back to a gentle boil. While the stock is coming to a boil, either hand-shred or chop the chicken into small pieces and put back into the pot.

For the Dumplin's

2 cups self-rising flour
2 heaping teaspoons baking powder
1/4 teaspoon baking soda
1 cup buttermilk
Salt and pepper to taste.

Sift the dry ingredients, except the baking soda. Make a "well" in the center. Mix baking soda and buttermilk and pour into the well. Gently mix until you get a soft, moist dough. Put onto a floured surface. Pinch off about an inch at a time, douse in flour, and drop in boiling stock, making sure to shake off the extra flour OVER the stock pot (this thickens and flavors the stock). Drop all the dough as quickly as you can, stirring frequently to avoid clumping. Dumplin's are done when they bob on the top. Serve hot. Makes 10 to16 servings.

NORA BOXER

Scrambled Eggs with Leeks, Mushrooms, and Feta

In the summer of 2006, when I returned to Taos after six months' travel in East Africa, I rented a new place, one that came with a chicken coop in the backyard. Since I was a long-time vegetable gardener, the coop seemed like a bonus: chickens were the hobby-agriculturalist's logical next step.

I hadn't even moved in yet when a barista in a café in town overheard me talking with my friend Kara about the possibility of keeping birds. "I have chickens!" the barista said. "They've been living in my Earthship, but I'm moving out of town. Do you want them?"

So four teenaged chickens moved in to the new place before I did. And Kara said, "It's funny how it works. You can ask the universe for true love, and you don't get it. But ask for chickens, and BOOM! There they are."

Thus I learned the joys and foibles of small-scale animal husbandry. Bless their hearts, the birds are all gone now. But we had a good run of it, my birds and I. This is how I used the majority of their eggs.

Nora Boxer is a fiction writer and a poet. She edited the 2006 and 2007 volumes of *Chokecherries* for SOMOS, and her work appears in the 2008 edition. She has also been a SOMOS Youth Mentor. She has returned to live in her other adopted home, the San Francisco Bay Area.

1 tablespoon unsalted butter (or Earth Balance)

4 eggs, beaten

1/2 of one medium leek, sliced lengthwise, washed well, and cut thinly

3-5 crimini mushrooms, sliced

4 ounces (about) good-quality feta cheese, crumbled

1 tablespoon milk (optional)

Salt and freshly ground pepper to taste

Over medium heat, melt butter in a large sauté pan and add salt and pepper. Add sliced leeks and sauté. When leeks are halfway cooked, add sliced mushrooms and continue cooking until the mushrooms and leeks are cooked to your liking.

Whisk the eggs (adding milk, if desired) and pour into the sauté pan. Stir and flip occasionally. When eggs are mostly cooked, add crumbled feta and continue to cook until fluffy. Serve as is, or with toast and jam or hash browns. Makes 2 servings.

Phyllis's Favorite Egg Foo Yung

In 1966 Julie and Jeff Tang bought the house across the street from us in Framingham, Massachusetts. They were a newly married couple from Taiwan who had met in graduate school.

Julie, an attractive young woman, thought she was an ugly duckling because in China she was considered too tall. She had majored in literature and wanted to be a writer, but her father insisted she take her master's in accounting. Every week, using a pseudonym, she sent an installment of a romance story to the Taipei newspaper feeling she'd betrayed literature.

Julie and I would drive to tiny Chinatown in Boston to shop for groceries, buy bakery sweet rolls and delicate almond cookies, and check out the roast ducks hanging in windows. She also taught me to cook some Chinese dishes. Mostly, I watched how she did it.

I had grown up in New York City thinking Cantonese was the only Chinese cuisine. Julie did Mandarin. I could make *bao tse*, scallion pancakes, easy stuff. Skins, wraps, were available. When I tried to shop without Julie and say the words, though, shopkeepers never understood me. Today I own five Chinese cookbooks, but this is the simple dish I make most often.

Phyllis Hotch is an award-winning poet who says she's watched SOMOS since 1987 widen to include not only the original summer series but also "the Winter Writers' Series, the mentorship programs, partners for homebound, and big programs with social impact for writers, censorship and peace."

EGG FOO YUNG

3 eggs, beaten
1/2 cup diced onions or scallions
1/2 cup diced roast pork or ham
1/2 cup (or more) vegetable oil
(Optional: sliced mushrooms and/or bean sprouts)

Combine eggs, onions, and meat. In a saucepan, over high heat, add oil; when hot, pour 1/2 of egg mixture into the pan. Brown for 2 minutes. Splash the top of the omelet with some hot oil, then flip the omelet over to complete cooking. Remove and drain on paper towels. Repeat for the remaining half of the egg mixture. Makes 2 servings.

69

Goin' Fishin'

Mama Fish soup. (Greek)

2 Potatoes split through
2 onions split through top twice
2 bay leaves
2 sticks celery
1½ l water
5 peppercorns
½ cup oil (slightly less)
1½ tsp salt or more
1 tomato slit
1 carrot cut in half

Start on high
simmer for
When ready
of fish in
for 8 min
before serv

Sauce for serving over fish.
½ cup oil
1 chopped green pepper
8 cloves garlic (less, chopped

Add fresh parsley
Add tin peeled tomatoes to 3
ripe tomatoes + fluid
1½ tsp black pepper
1 tsp salt
1 tsp sugar
Add water as necessary

70

71

LYN BLEILER

Sardine in Soar, or Marinated Sardines

Should you find yourself living in Venice near the Rialto *pescheria*, prepare to be awakened by the sound of seagulls squabbling over the fishing boats they escort to market each dawn. Morning after luxurious morning, I'd lay awake listening to their antics and marvel at the miracle of waking in a lair-like loft with yet another full day of Venetian magic spread out before me like a velvet carpet.

Unlike camera-toting summer tourists, winter *pescheria*-goers are primarily well dressed Italians, buttoned up in Burberry coats, many with stylish dogs. The market assumes a carnival-like atmosphere of playful banter as fishmongers barter over a dizzying array of fresh seafood, some of which, like gargantuan octopuses wriggling on beds of ice, are a tad too fresh for my taste.

By mid-afternoon, the ancient stone pavilion is silent again, barren of fish, fishmongers and fixtures—an empty theater set—except for seagulls or, as I think of them, the cleanup crew. Diligent workers, they scavenge the market floor until nary a mussel can be found, before flying off to wherever it is they fly off to. Only to reappear at dawn the next morning, just as their predecessors have for centuries.

Lyn Bleiler, a published poet and freelance writer, has been assistant to the director of SOMOS for four years. She is the author of *Taos* (Arcadia Publishing) and was a writer in residence at the Emily Harvey Foundation in Venice, Italy, in 2009 and 2011.

1 pound 2 ounces fresh sardines (preferably from the Rialto Fish Market)

2-1/2 cups finely sliced white onions

2 cups sunflower (or canola) oil

1/4 cup white wine vinegar

1/3 cup plus 1 tablespoon extra virgin olive oil

1/4 cup golden raisins

3 tablespoons pine nuts

3 tablespoons all-purpose flour

2 teaspoons salt

Have your fishmonger remove sardines' heads, scales and innards. Wash thoroughly and pat dry with paper towel. Dust with flour. In a non-stick pan, place onions in 2 ounces (1/4 cup) of water, and add sunflower oil and salt. Cook over high heat for five minutes while stirring. Add vinegar and cook for five more minutes. Crush raisins and add to the pan along with pine nuts. Cook for two minutes then remove from heat to cool. (Onions should be cooked al dente.)

In a sauté pan, cook floured sardines in a small amount of hot oil until golden. Remove from oil and place on paper towel to cool. In a terrine, place layer of onions, then a layer of sardines and a pinch of salt. Repeat layering, finishing with a layer of onions on top. Set aside to marinate for at least 24 hours. Makes 4 servings.

CHRISTINA LUCIA PERALTA-RAMOS

Hard Clams Kanawha

My grandmother Millicent Rogers is well known as one of America's most glamorous style icons. But what is not so well known is that she was also a homebody and loving mother.

One of her hobbies was collecting and cataloging over 1,500 of our family's recipes, some dating back to the 1600's, when our ancestors immigrated to America on the Mayflower.

Many of the recipes have amusing names, taken from family members, places and various homes. Clams Kanawha, for example, is from the estate of my great-great-grandfather, Henry Huttleston Rogers. H. H. Rogers was one of the founders of Standard Oil, and Kanawha was his magnificent racing yacht.

On the Kanawha, family and close friends, such as Mark Twain, John Rockefeller, and William Vanderbilt, dined in regal splendor on the high seas. Though that is a time long gone by, thanks to my grandmother my family has enjoyed these delicious recipes for generations. I am delighted to now share this one with fellow gourmets.

Christina Lucia Peralta-Ramos is the granddaughter of Millicent Rogers and daughter of Paul Peralta-Ramos, founder of the Millicent Rogers Museum in Taos. Christina has been a fashion model since she was a child growing up in New York City and is presently spokeswoman for the Millicent Rogers Museum, where she is starting an archives department with the hundreds of photographs she has inherited of her grandmother.

6 tablespoons Mornay sauce (see note below)

2 teaspoons Worcestershire sauce

1 teaspoon chopped fresh parsley

4 teaspoons grated Parmesan cheese

1/2 teaspoon celery salt

1/2 teaspoon paprika

1 salt spoon (about 1/8 teaspoon) cayenne

2 cups finely chopped fresh clams

8 tablespoons fried breadcrumbs

Heat the sauce, add the Worcestershire, parsley, 2 teaspoons Parmesan, celery salt, paprika and cayenne. As soon as the cheese is melted, stir in the clams and breadcrumbs. Place filling in large clamshells, sprinkle with the remaining cheese and brown in a moderate oven. Makes 6 to 8 first-course servings.

(Editor's note: Mornay sauce is a classic white sauce [Béchamel] to which grated Gruyere cheese has been added.)

SCOTT CONTI

Calamari for Emeril

Not long after leaving culinary school in 1996, I worked in Biloxi, on the strip of Gulf Coast casinos. The Beau Rivage hired me as chef for the new Coast Brew Pub. Mississippi was a challenge for an Easterner like me, but the restaurant was a success.

One day my server came into the kitchen and said, "There's a guy out there, some chef, who wants you to come to his table." Another cook who felt compelled to critique? I had an attitude as I strode out. As I got closer a slightly familiar face called out, "Hey, chef, how're ya doin'?" Ohmygod, I thought. It's Emeril Lagasse! Next thought: I'm going to have to feed him!

We talked. He ordered. Later, Emeril complimented me on the calamari dish and said, "Keep up the good work." Needless to say, I was floating on air. And speaking of floating... after I left Biloxi, hurricane Katrina hit. The Beau Rivage complex was completely destroyed. When the storm subsided, slot machines and plates were seen bobbing all over the water. But my memory of that brief time has not floated away.

The following recipe is for one Emeril-size serving.

Scott Conti changed his life in young middle age and graduated from the Cordon Bleu Ecole in Scottsdale, Arizona, in 1996. He lives in Las Vegas, Nevada. He is a fan of SOMOS, poets, writers, and cookbooks.

FRIED CALAMARI

4 ounces calamari (squid) tubes and tentacles, cleaned well ("ink eye" removed)
1 pint buttermilk
1/2 cup all-purpose flour
A pinch each of finely ground salt, white pepper, and Old Bay seasoning
Lemon zest and wedges for garnish
Spicy marinara sauce (purchased or homemade)

Cut calamari tubes 1/4-inch thick. If tentacles are large, cut in half. Soak in buttermilk to coat. Place calamari in a perforated pan or colander to drain. Remove, dredge in flour seasoned with salt, pepper, and Old Bay; toss until evenly coated. Set aside.

Set up a pan (preferably cast iron), with 1 inch of vegetable oil and heat to about 350 degrees. Use tongs or a spatula to carefully move calamari around in the oil. Cook in small batches until golden brown. Remove from pan, drain on paper towels. If desired, add salt at this time. Place on plate.

Garnish cooked calamari with lemon zest and place lemon wedges on the side; serve with ramekin of spiced marinara sauce, and, as Emeril would say, "*Bam!*"

ELIZABETH BURNS

Tilapia à la Talpa

I love to cook, but my bookshelves aren't groaning with cookbooks. I don't watch cooking shows or read food magazines. I found the "Eat" in *Eat, Pray, Love* tedious. I was born into a non-foodie family. My mother has many talents, but cooking isn't one of them. Her culinary failures, rather than her successes, are the stuff of family legend. Growing up, I never spent time in the kitchen with her learning generations-old family recipes.

Our dinners, though, were always home-cooked and the servings generous. Unless Mom was on a diet, in which case we all went on starvation rations. Now that it's only her and my father, she spends little time in the kitchen; she finds it's not inspiring to cook for a man who can't tell the difference between Two-Buck Chuck and Chateau Margaux. When she does cook, my mother strictly follows a recipe, levels every teaspoon.

So I had to discover the joy of cooking on my own. Unlike my mother, I see a recipe as a sketch to be completed my way. More often, I invent a dish. Now if my mother and I are in the kitchen together, I am the one teaching her. This is one of my creations that is one of her favorites.

Elizabeth Burns, author of the memoir *The Silken Thread*, lives on a small farm in Talpa, New Mexico, with two horses, four goats, twenty chickens, several thousand bees and one boyfriend. She is a friend of SOMOS.

SAUTÉED TILAPIA WITH PEPPERS AND KUMQUATS

2 (or more) tablespoons of butter

1/2 teaspoon (or so) coriander seeds

1/2 teaspoon (or so) cumin seeds

1/2 cup diced onions

1 handful of kumquats, cut in half

1/2 red bell pepper, diced

1 small tomato, diced

6-8 Brussels sprouts, separated into leaves

4 medium tilapia fillets

Juice of 1/2 lemon

Salt to taste

Melt the butter in a large skillet over medium heat. Add the cumin and coriander seeds and heat them for about two minutes. Add the onions and sauté them for another three minutes. Add the kumquats and red pepper; sauté until the peppers soften a bit. Add the tomatoes and sprout leaves. Sauté for two more minutes. Push mixture to the sides of the skillet. Put in the tilapia fillets, adding more butter if necessary. Dust the fillets with salt and douse everything with lemon juice. Cooking time for the fillets will depend on their size; when they flake, they are done. Serve over steamed rice. Makes 4 servings.

BOB PARKER

Stuffed Sole with Pernod

Returning from a fishing trip on the Dean River in northern British Colombia in 1979, my friends and I arrived back in Vancouver to find that our hostess had invited more guests for dinner, but with no idea what to fix. As conservationists, we fishermen had left the Steelhead to carry out their life's mission up river. Thus we'd arrived empty handed.

I said, "Let's go down to the wharf in Deep Cove and see if there is any seafood. I might have an idea, if I can cook in your kitchen." Fresh caught sole and a bucket of crab legs were what we carried back home.

I had cooked sole for years, sautéed gently in butter with parsley; but our hostess was hoping for something a little more grandiose. Hmmm... Could the sole and crab be combined for a gourmet dish?

"Put on the rice, crack the crab and, by the way, do you have red pepper, green onions, capers, breadcrumbs and Pernod for a delicate, distinctive flavor?" I asked. I then proceeded to make a crab stuffing for the rolled, baked sole, served on a bed of moist rice. This recipe has become a memorable dish I have served for decades.

Bob Parker, a friend and fan of SOMOS, is an architect, artist, cook and longtime resident of Taos.

1 pound fresh sole fillets (about 2 fillets, medium size, for each person)

For the Stuffing

Mix the following and keep in the refrigerator until ready:

1 tin high quality chunk crabmeat, drained of excess liquid

1/2 red bell pepper chopped fine

4 green onions chopped fine

1/2 cup fine breadcrumbs

1 whole egg

2 tablespoons capers

1/4 cup grated Parmesan cheese

Paprika for sprinkling

4 tablespoons of Pernod

Coarse ground pepper to taste

Precook 1 cup basmati rice with 1/2 cup wild rice and set aside. Preheat oven to 400 degrees. Place a small amount of stuffing on each fillet, roll to seal and turn over to hold ends in place. Place each fillet on a buttered baking pan.

Sprinkle 1/4 cup Parmesan cheese and paprika over each fillet prior to baking. Any additional stuffing may be placed around the fillets. If desired, sprinkle more Pernod over the fillets. Bake about 20 minutes or until bubbly. Serve over the rice mixture and garnish with baking liquid and chopped chives. Makes 4 servings.

BARBARA SCOTT

Promises en Papillote

The kitchen is not my domain, but I'd been promising my fiancé Michael I'd start cooking as soon as I earned my MA from St. John's College in Santa Fe in May. So when my friend Bonnie invited me over for salmon en papillote one evening, I paid careful attention to how she prepared it—especially the way she julienned the vegetables with her cleaver. A couple of weeks later, I even went to Monet's Kitchen here in Taos and bought a sushi knife, a rather fancy cleaver.

Every week I promised Michael I'd make him the delicious salmon dinner. But as each Friday rolled around, Michael could tell I was tired and stressed by work and studies, so he generously offered to take me out to dinner.

In the meantime, my friend Rick broke the news that he was moving from Taos to Gallup. He's such a special friend that I didn't want to see him go without getting together for a last supper. I suggested he pick a restaurant, and I'd go along with his choice. Instead, he asked if we could just have dinner at my house.

So after about three weeks of reneging on my promise to cook a nice salmon dinner for Michael, I made it for another man, Rick. He said it was perfectly cooked, juicy and flavorful.

I still haven't made the dish for Michael. In fact, I've quit promising.

Barbara Scott, a big fan of SOMOS, is owner of Final Eyes, an editorial-services firm: www.finaleyes.net, barb@finaleyes.net.

SALMON EN PAPILLOTE

Butter a large circle of parchment paper or aluminum foil, about 15 inches in diameter. Lay one small salmon fillet (one serving) on the paper, right of center. Spread the salmon with butter and sprinkle with sliced vegetables, such as carrots, red pepper, summer squash, or French green beans. Season with salt and pepper, freshly squeezed lemon juice and/or white wine. Top with a pat of butter. Fold parchment or foil into papillote (paper case) and seal the edges, like a calzone. Place on a cookie sheet and bake for 10 to 15 minutes at 400–425 degrees, or until puffed. Serve each person an individual papillote (unopened), with a small pair of sharp scissors, to open the cases themselves and savor the steamy aroma.

(Barb's note: This recipe was taken almost directly from Bonnie Black's memoir, *How to Cook a Crocodile*. Only the name, and one or two of the vegetables, have been changed.)

BILL DUFRESNE

Bill's Planked Salmon

When I came to Taos in '95, I went ice fishing with Leo, a local meat cutter from Cid's Food Market. Leo and I went to Eagle Nest Lake in January, drilled our holes, and fished for lake salmon. We always caught salmon.

After Leo moved away, there was no ice fishing for me for years. Then my friend Andrew and I decided to try it. He is from Hong Kong, and I am from the Hudson Valley. Without Leo, we floundered. Every January for four years we drove to the ice in Andrew's old Jeep. Not bad if the sun was out and no wind. We did not catch salmon. We only caught cold.

On the last year we drilled our holes and fished, the sun went in, and the wind blew. It got really cold. The wind blew harder, and it got colder. And the wind kept blowing. We tried to outlast each other, but finally we quit. No salmon. That was the end of our ice fishing. I went to Smith's and bought salmon and cooked it this way: on Cedar planks.

Bill Dufresne is a retired attorney, resident of Taos, and friend of SOMOS.

6 ounces boned, skinned salmon per person
(Bill recommends farm-raised Atlantic salmon because it is thicker
and has more fat)

Cedar planks (untreated) — soaked for 12 to 24 hours in water
(Bill puts them in a container and weighs them down with a rock)

Your favorite marinade
(Bill uses soy and honey)

Two hours before cooking, place the salmon portions in a large Ziploc bag and add your marinade of choice. Seal bag and place in the refrigerator. When ready to cook, heat your grill to high. Place the salmon on the planks (do not let salmon overhang). Place the planks on the grill. Cover. Do not turn or move the salmon. Cook 10 to 20 minutes. Feel the salmon with your forefinger to test for firmness. Remove and serve for a soft pink middle or leave on the grill for well done. Discard the plank.

PRUDENCE HAWTHORNE ABELN

Teacher's Hot-Dish

Growing up in the fifties in a suburb of Minneapolis, the big event for me during grade school was the day we invited our teacher home for lunch. As the youngest of four daughters, I often shared the same teacher who had previously taught my older sisters. And each of our Wooddale School teachers had also enjoyed one of Mom's home cooked meals when my sisters had invited her home for that special day.

Every year, Mom would let us choose what we wanted her to prepare for our teacher's lunch. The dish I always selected was called "Teacher's Hot-Dish." As a favorite of mine, I was sure that my teacher would feel the same way. What I hadn't figured out was that the casserole got its name because each of my sisters before me had chosen the same meal for their teachers.

So I now imagine that the teachers at Wooddale School probably compared notes and decided that my mom only knew how to cook one casserole—"Teacher's Hot-Dish." Although the recipe is very simple, this remains one of my kids' favorites when they come home for a visit. See if this doesn't take you back to the 1950s.

SOMOS board member Prudence Abeln is a "corporate escapee" who now owns the Dreamcatcher B&B in Taos with her husband, John. She has been a teacher, trainer, magazine circulation promotion manager, mortgage loan officer and consummate community volunteer.

TUNA CASSEROLE (1)

2 cans Campbell's cream of mushroom soup
1 large can (or bag) chow mein noodles (about 4 cups)
2 eggs (separated)
1 large (12-ounce) can white albacore tuna (drained)

Preheat oven to 375 degrees. Using 1 -1/3 cans soup (add water to make 2 cups), heat the soup in a saucepan. Add the chow mein noodles and egg yolks and stir well. Then add tuna and pour the mixture into a large meatloaf pan. Beat the egg whites and fold them into the tuna mixture.

Bake at 375 degrees for 45 minutes. Before serving, heat remaining soup (stretching it with a little milk) to use as a sauce. Makes 3 to 4 servings.

T. MARTIN-HART

Classic Tuna Casserole

My Southern parents were blessed with five children. As the middle child, I often volunteered to help in the kitchen. To this day, nothing stirs up tastier memories than family dinners of old.

My mother was a master chef. She taught us how to cook even before we were tall enough to clear the counter. "Watch everything I do," she instructed. "I want you to learn how to properly feed yourselves and others." Brandishing her knife, she whacked an onion in half and feverishly chopped away.

Daddy insisted on keeping leftovers, but he would never eat them. Mother wanted to throw leftovers away, but she always ate them. Like Jack Spratt and his wife, their sixty-five-year marriage was destined to survive.

One evening when Mother prepared an old family classic, tuna casserole, Daddy took one bite and said, "Something's missing."

"But," the master chef defended, "it's the same as always."

Later, as we cleaned the kitchen, Mother burst out laughing when she saw the unopened can of tuna on the counter. She'd forgotten to add it.

T. Martin-Hart, a friend of SOMOS, is a writer and public relations specialist serving up culinary delights in her Avondale Estates, Georgia, cottage.

TUNA CASSEROLE (2)

1 small to medium onion, chopped
1-2 tablespoons butter
1-2 cans tuna or albacore, drained
1 can cream of mushroom soup
1/3-1/2 cup milk
1 small box elbow macaroni (about 8 ounces)
Salt and pepper to taste

(Optional additions: chopped artichoke hearts, peas, carrots, pimiento, capers, chopped tomatoes, etc.)

(Topping possibilities: crushed potato chips, grated cheddar cheese and French-fried onion rings)

Preheat oven to 350 degrees. Sauté onion in butter. Add soup and milk. Stir in tuna. (If desired, add a small amount of optional ingredients.) Cook macaroni according to package directions; drain and add to tuna mixture. Pour into a buttered, 2-quart casserole dish. Add topping of choice. Cover loosely with foil and bake about 20 minutes. Makes 4 to 6 servings.

Veggie Medleys

SPINACH TART

CRUST: 300g (500ml) COOKED ...
2 EGG WHITES, LIGHTLY WHISKED.

FILLING: 300g (350ml) COOKED SPINACH, FINEL[Y]
HALF TUB (125g) SMOOTH COTTAGE CHEE[SE]
125ml PLAIN YOGHURT
2 EXTRA LARGE EGGS, WHISKED
JUICE & RIND GRATED OF ½ LEMON
SALT & PEPPER
100g (250ml) CHEDDAR CHEESE, FINE[LY]

METHOD: PREHEAT THE OVEN TO 180°C (350°[F])
SHALLOW OVEN-PROOF DISH WITH M[?]
MIX THE RICE & EGG WHITES & LIN[E T?]
MIXTURE, BRINGING WELL UP ON [SIDE]
COTTAGE CHEESE, YOGURT & WHISK[?]
BOWL & MIX THOROUGHLY. SEASON
RIND & SALT/PEPPER TO TASTE
SPOON THE FILLING INTO THE C[?]
THE CHEESE ON TOP. PLACE [?]
FOR ABOUT 30 MINS OR [JU?]
HAS SET.

MEAT/ C[?]

90

ALEXANDRA PIETRASANTA ROSE

Russian Eggplant Caviar

It was my first Russian Easter in America in 1950. My widowed mother and I had recently arrived from Italy, and although my mother spoke fluent English, French, Italian, and Russian, I was confined to Italian, French, and one sentence in English ("I like chocolate"), which I had learned when the American soldiers arrived in 1945. Fortunately, my Russian relatives all spoke French.

My grandfather, Prince Vladimir Troubetzkoy, the doyen of the White Russian community in New York City, always celebrated Russian Easter with an elaborate feast featuring pasha, koulich, and eggplant caviar. He used to say, "The days of caviar are over for us, but we still have our own special caviar."

He taught me the recipe, and I made it with my mother for that first Russian Easter in America. It has always received accolades.

Alexandra Pietrasanta Rose and her husband Peter Rose are new members of SOMOS who have recently moved to Taos on a permanent basis from New York City. She has worked for the Gallimard publishing house in France and has been published in *Connoisseur Magazine*.

EGGPLANT CAVIAR

2 eggplants
4 large yellow onions, peeled and chopped
5-6 tomatoes, chopped
1/2 cup olive oil
1 tablespoon whole peppercorns
1 bay leaf
2 teaspoons salt
2 tablespoons cider vinegar
Sugar to taste

Bake whole, unpeeled eggplants in a 350-degree oven for 1-1/2 hours. Sauté onions until slightly browned. Chop the inside of the eggplants and add to onions, along with chopped tomatoes, bay leaf, salt and pepper, and cook until most of the liquid is evaporated (about a half hour). Mix in the vinegar and sugar and place in a 2-quart earthenware dish in a 250-degree oven for a half hour, then turn oven off and leave it in the oven for at least 6 hours or overnight. Delicious as a sandwich or appetizer spread. Makes enough spread for 20 appetizers.

VICTORIA MACQUEEN

Layered Cheese Appetizer

After having been invited to an event, I offered to bring an appetizer. About 9 p.m. the night before the event, though, I remembered I'd forgotten my offer. Uh oh. What to do?

I raced into the kitchen in search of something. I opened the fridge and pulled things out that might just go together: cheese, nuts, roasted peppers, pesto, and seasonings. *Wow.* It looked like a cheese ball or log in the making. Instead, I decided to layer all these ingredients and hope for the best.

The next day I plated my appetizer, and to my surprise it looked good. All the colors and textures made for a pretty presentation. It seemed all the guests were enjoying it, too. It was the first dish to disappear. I even had requests for the recipe.

My layered cheese "surprise" has been a hit at many events ever since.

Victoria MacQueen, a longtime friend of SOMOS, was born and raised in Taos, where she and her husband also raised their family.

1, 8-ounce block of cream cheese, softened

1/2 cup sharp cheddar cheese, shredded

1 teaspoon dry ranch dressing powder mix (or seasoning of your choice)

1/4 -1/2 cup nuts (pine nuts, or any type will do), chopped

1/2 cup marinated artichoke hearts, drained

1/2 cup roasted red peppers, drained and chopped

1/4-1/2 cup pesto

Line a 2-cup, round-bottom bowl with plastic wrap, enough to fold over the rim. Mix cheeses with seasoning until well blended. Divide cheese mixture into thirds.

Sprinkle 1/2 of the nuts into the bottom of the bowl. Working with wet hands, form a round, flat pancake shape with 1/3 of the cheese mixture. Place this over nuts. Spread with half of artichoke, pesto, nuts and peppers, in layers.

Repeat with cheese and the rest of the ingredients. Finish with cheese. Seal edges and wrap tightly. Refrigerate overnight. Before serving, invert onto a large plate and surround with crackers or vegetables. Makes enough for a small gathering.

HEIDI SIEG-SMITH

Wild Mushroom Ragout

My mother bought wild mushrooms in the grocery store when I was growing up in Berlin in the 1950s. But while she prepared a mushroom dish, she usually told stories about finding wild mushrooms in the woods when she was younger.

When I was living in Vermont's Green Mountains in the '70s and '80s, my mother went mushroom hunting with us whenever she came to visit. She was the expert who knew where to look for our favorite chanterelles and boletus.

The entire family spent many hours in the cool forest, fanning out in all directions, hoping for a bountiful harvest. After admiring each other's finds, we hurried home in anticipation of a scrumptious mushroom dinner.

Mom went straight to the kitchen and started cooking. She didn't measure anything. "Take a handful of this, and pinch of that," was her running commentary. I watched carefully, making mental notes on how her amounts might translate into a recipe.

Remembering those afternoons, I can still smell the damp moss under the canopy of fir trees and the mouthwatering aroma in the kitchen while the ragout simmered. Mushroom hunting and then making this ragout are among our family's most treasured memories.

Heidi Sieg-Smith, SOMOS member, writer, landscape painter and gardener, turns to mushroom hunting in Taos come July. She is the author of the memoir, *After the Bombs: My Berlin*.

2 tablespoons unsalted butter, or more if needed

1/4-inch slice of pancetta, chopped into small cubes

1 large onion, diced

1 pound chanterelles or other wild mushrooms, cleaned and quartered

2 tablespoons all-purpose flour

1 cup vegetable broth

Salt and freshly ground pepper to taste

6 tablespoons chopped parsley, divided

2 tablespoons sour cream

Sauté pancetta in melted butter over medium heat in a wide pan until slightly browned. Add onions and sauté until translucent. Add mushrooms, sauté for approximately 5 minutes. Dust mixture evenly with flour and stir until all moisture is absorbed. Add more butter if all seems too dry. Add the broth and gently stir until mixture starts bubbling. Add salt, pepper and 4 tablespoons parsley. Turn heat to low, cover and simmer for about 20 minutes. In a cup or small bowl, mix sour cream with a bit of the liquid from the ragout until smooth; add to ragout. Bring to a simmer again and cook for about 5 minutes. Adjust seasonings. Garnish with remaining parsley before serving. Makes 4 to 6 servings.

(Heidi's note: This dish works just as well with generic mushrooms.)

Grandma Marchese's Sicilian Potato Patties

Concetta and Salvatore Marchese settled in Poughkeepsie, New York, from Palermo and central Sicily around 1910. Salvatore (Toto) was a stonemason who directed the brickwork construction at Vassar College in the 1920s and 1930s. Concetta knew from her youth in the village of Mussomelli that potatoes were cheap and went a long way for a growing family.

Occasionally, while grandma choreographed meals in her kitchen, Toto snagged steaks or sausages and took me, his young grandson, down to the basement where, sitting on stools in front of the furnace, he grilled them until they were charred. Surrounding shelves contained home-canned tomatoes from their summer garden and a gigantic oak wine barrel filled with good red table wine. When we brought the well-done meats upstairs, the family had gathered and potato patties and other delicious dishes were enjoyed at a long dining table.

This recipe has passed through four generations of creative cooks and has become legendary. Make lots. They can be eaten warm or cold, keep well, and are a nice addition to a large casual dinner party or buffet.

Ron Marchese Ciancio is a painter who is now making steel stabiles in his Taos studio. Over the years he has supported various SOMOS publications and programs through his art. He has also been known to cook for writers.

SICILIAN POTATO PATTIES

5-6 pounds of russet potatoes
(depending on how many you plan to feed), washed, peeled, and quartered
Good olive oil
2-3 yellow onions, peeled and diced
3-4 eggs
Italian breadcrumbs
1 cup or more of freshly grated Parmesan or Romano cheese
1 bunch of Italian parsley
Several cloves of garlic, peeled and left whole

Cook potatoes in boiling salted water until not quite as soft as mashed. Drain. Set aside to cool while preparing additional ingredients. Sauté onions in some olive oil until transparent. Chop a handful of the parsley and set aside. Mash potatoes until crumbly, not smooth, add whole eggs and other ingredients (except garlic) until you feel they are well blended and the amounts of ingredients are balanced. Mix together. Shape into oblong patties approximately 4" wide x 1/2" thick. Lightly brown garlic cloves in a generous amount of olive oil in a heavy frying pan, over medium heat. Cook patties, first one side and then the other, until a nice golden-brown color. Do not burn. Add additional oil as required. Remove, drain on paper towels. Makes 8 to 14 servings.

GALE PICARD DORION

Sweet Potato Pot Luck

Friday morning, very early. Tonight, Shabbat dinner gathering. Pot luck. Fish already spoken for, same with desert. Maybe a vegetable dish? Love squash. How about squash?

It's a treasured group of friends tonight. Want them to feel cared for. Nobody relegated to remainders! What's in the fridge? *Ooops*, not much! No squash. No fresh veggies. No way frozen veggies!

Searching among random foods for fresh, taste-bud-opening sensations. Hmm ... oh dear ... oh yeah ... got it! Sweet potatoes—not yams—fresh ginger, and, oh look, apples. Crunchy Gala apples. My mouth starts watering. My eyes brighten. My heart opens. *Yes!*

Gale Picard Dorion is a Taos jeweler, painter, lover of words and sounds, storyteller, and member of SOMOS.

7 sweet potatoes (not yams), washed well
1 small fresh ginger root, peeled
1 Gala (or other crunchy) apple
Olive oil
Himalayan salt (or brand of choice)
Sprig of parsley, or other green leaf herb

Place sweet potatoes in a baking dish and cover with foil or a lid. Bake at 450 degrees until really soft, about an hour. Allow to cool enough to handle.

Grate ginger and sauté in a little olive oil. Add salt to taste. Scoop the insides of the soft sweet potatoes into the sautéed ginger and stir well.

Put sweet potatoes and ginger in mixing bowl. Add peeled, minced apple and fold in. Serve in a bowl of contrasting color. Garnish with sprig of leafy green herb. Share. Makes 8 servings.

DORI VINELLA

Hashbrown Heaven

For twenty-four years, while raising three sons, I ran Dori's—a small bakery-turned-café next to the Taos Post Office. It was a funky, downhome Taos place where locals kept personalized ceramic mugs on the wall and where an old upright piano allowed spontaneous music to fill the air. It was a favorite hangout for writers—many of whom, like Julia Cameron and Christine Autumn, have mentioned Dori's in their memoirs. Just about the time Dori's was becoming established, Taos's own John Nichols was gaining national recognition, after Robert Redford made a movie from John's book *The Milagro Beanfield War*.

Fame never went to John's head. He stayed the same generous, unassuming guy. Most days, he would pick up his mail at the post office, walk over to Dori's, and settle in to "his" alcove, where he'd write for hours, often on the back of envelopes or whatever mail had come that day. Before long, tourists began to show up asking if "the" John Nichols really hung out here. There were many times when John would be sitting right there, just a few feet away, in a rumpled shirt and baggy khakis—looking like anything but a successful writer. I'd lean over the counter and reply, "You know, he does stop by now and then. But I never know when he'll come in."

In 1997, after a good long run, it was time to close Dori's. John was my last customer. This was his favorite dish.

Dori Vinella has lived in Taos for over forty years and has been the executive director at SOMOS for fourteen years. As another endeavor, she makes and markets "Seasons of Taos" gourmet seasonings. Go to her website www.seasonsoftaos.com for more information.

HASHBROWN POTATOES

1 tablespoon each of butter and olive oil
2 cups grated, cooked russet potatoes
1/3-1/2 cup grated cheddar cheese
1/4 cup chopped green chile (medium or hot)
1 egg
Dash of Dori's Seasonings Chile Original (see Dori's bio, left)
Dash of garlic powder to taste
Sprig of parsley

In a hot frying pan, add the butter and olive oil, then the potatoes and brown them on both sides. Add chile, seasonings, and cheese and cook until cheese is melted. In a separate pan, cook egg over easy, or as you like it. Place egg on top and serve with parsley garnish. Makes 1 hungry-man serving.

CATHERINE STRISIK

Fried Eggplant Sandwiches

For one weekend each summer in the 1960s, Yiayia and Papou would pack up their Oldsmobile with suitcases of old clothes, vegetables from their garden, and me, and drive three hours from their Greek neighborhood in Haverhill, Massachusetts, to Thea Lemonia Bargas' Greek neighborhood in Bridgeport, Connecticut.

From the moment Thea opened her door to greet us with her raspy basil-scented breath, I knew from her floured apron and the spitting and splattering behind her what awaited us in her kitchen, where no one spoke English and no one spoke softly. All the sounds—chewing of eggplant, swallowing of eggplant, and digesting of eggplant—were in Greek. Even as a child, I was sure defecation of eggplant, purple-robed, round-thighed, and thick-hipped, would be in Greek, too.

At Thea's table, the oily soft meat of the fried eggplant spilled out from the edges of the bread and dripped onto our chins and fingers. This was a time when licking our fingers and being noisy at it were allowed. Here at her kitchen table with my immigrant family, I couldn't tell the difference between one Greek and another. It was as if we each descended from Alexander, like Papou always said. Eating fried eggplant sandwiches, I believed him.

Poet Catherine Strisik, author of *Thousand-Cricket Song,* has been active in Taos's poetry community for nearly thirty years. A member of SOMOS, she has read at various times for SOMOS's Winter Writers' Series.

1 large eggplant, washed, unpeeled, and sliced 1/4-inch thick
1 cup all-purpose flour
1/4 cup grated Kefaloteri or Parmesan cheese
Salt
2 eggs, beaten
1 cup olive oil for frying

Sprinkle eggplant slices generously with salt and let stand in a colander to drain for 15 minutes. Rinse well with cold water and pat dry. Dip in combined flour and cheese, coating both sides, then dip in egg. Repeat with each slice. Fry in hot oil until light brown on both sides, about 10 minutes. Serve with sauce (below). Makes 3 servings.

Yogurt Sauce

Blend together:
1 cup Greek lowfat yogurt
1 teaspoon red wine vinegar
1 clove garlic
1/2 teaspoon each of dry mustard, oregano, and salt
A dash of pepper

Refrigerate for one hour before serving.

LUCY HERRMAN

Imam Bayildi, or The Priest Fainted

Like most Greek families, mine enjoyed one or more meatless dinners each week. The creativity displayed by numerous hearty vegetable main courses is a testament to Greek ingenuity. My family often drew on Turkish influences, as we were from Thessaloniki in Greek Macedonia near the Turkish border.

This dish was said to have been served to the local imam, who found it so good that he fainted. I have created my own version of this dish, which traditionally has eggplant and a great deal more olive oil.

Lucy Herrman is a Taos artist and writer. She is also a former cooking teacher who has regularly written a newspaper food column. Lucy has recently discovered SOMOS and its programs. She says, "SOMOS is an example of why Taos is such an amazing place!"

GREEK VEGETABLE CASSEROLE

2 medium onions, thinly sliced

1 red and 1 green pepper, cored, seeded and thinly sliced

2 medium zucchini, thinly sliced in diagonal rounds

2 medium potatoes, scrubbed, cut in half and thinly sliced

4 fresh tomatoes, thinly sliced

About 6 tablespoons olive oil, divided

12 small sprigs of fresh thyme

Salt and freshly ground pepper to taste

Preheat oven to 425 degrees. In a medium bowl, toss the onions with a tablespoon of olive oil. Spread on the bottom of a heavy baking dish, such as a ceramic-lined cast iron pan like Le Creuset. Add the peppers to the bowl with another tablespoon of olive oil. Toss well and distribute over the onions. Add the zucchini to the bowl with another tablespoon of olive oil and toss well. Add to the peppers in a single layer. Sprinkle with salt and pepper.

Add the potatoes to the bowl with another tablespoon of olive oil. Toss well and layer on top of the zucchini. Sprinkle with salt and pepper. Layer the tomatoes on top of the potatoes. With your hands, press down to flatten the vegetables a little. Decoratively arrange the thyme sprigs on top, sprinkle with salt and pepper, and drizzle any remaining oil over the tomatoes. Cover pan with foil.

Bake at 425 degrees for about 20 to 30 minutes, or until the potatoes are tender when pierced. Remove the foil and bake about 20 to 30 more minutes or until the potatoes are browned and the tomatoes are somewhat shriveled. Total cooking time should be 45 to 60 minutes. Serve with a Greek salad and crusty bread. Makes 4 to 6 main course servings, 8 to 10 side dish servings.

HOLLY AZZARI

Torta de Zucchina, or Squash Pie

Though we shared the same birthday, my Italian mother-in-law and I were nothing alike. We loved the same cute guy, though, so we found a way to coexist, despite the fact that we had different faiths (she had one and I didn't), different political views (I had one and she didn't), different sensibilities (more than just a generation gap), and personalities so opposite that it is a wonder we loved the same cute guy.

She had learned to cook by spending years in her mother-in-law's kitchen. As an insufferable young woman, I would have rather asked her for beauty tips than ask her to teach me how to cook.

When it became evident that he couldn't live without some of his mom's dishes, I relented and asked her for recipes, of which there were none. My worst fears had materialized: I would have to observe her in her own kitchen while I attempted to write down ingredients and measurements. This was an episode of "Everybody Loves Raymond" long before everybody loved Raymond.

I've been married to her son for forty-eight years, and she's been gone for the last fifteen. But with a modicum of maturity I now respect and appreciate her silent acceptance of things so alien to her, her unspoken disappointment in our choices, and her legacy of those delicious recipes.

Holly Azzari of Arroyo Seco is a retired legislative aide and political campaign coordinator from Los Angeles. A supporter of SOMOS, she now calls herself "a political junkie and professional slug."

2 pounds zucchini (unpeeled), sliced

1 onion, chopped

3 cloves garlic, minced

1 tablespoon dried oregano

2 tablespoons minced fresh basil (or 1 tablespoon dried)

2-3 tablespoons olive oil

4 eggs, beaten

3/4 cup grated fresh Parmesan or Romano cheese

3/4 cup breadcrumbs

1 small bunch Italian parsley, chopped

1 small can tomato sauce

1/4 cup (1/2 stick) unsalted butter, cut in dice

Salt and freshly ground pepper to taste

Preheat oven to 375 degrees. Grease a 9 x 14-inch Pyrex dish. In a large sauté pan, with just enough oil to cover bottom, cook the zucchini, onion, garlic, herbs, parsley, salt and pepper until 3/4 done (still crisp, not soggy). Add the tomato sauce and continue cooking until zucchini is tender.

Pour mixture into a large mixing bowl. Stir in the eggs and most of the cheese and breadcrumbs, to reach drop-biscuit consistency. Adjust seasoning as necessary. Spread mixture in Pyrex dish. Dot with butter and the remaining cheese and breadcrumbs. Bake about 35 to 40 minutes, until the bottom is browned and the top is golden brown. Allow to cool slightly before cutting. Can be served warm or cold. Makes 24, 2-inch squares.

ELLEN WOOD

Halushkies, or Czech Dumplings With Onions

Right after her parents got off the boat from Czechoslovakia, my mother was born. My grandparents settled in Pennsylvania and had twelve more children. Feeding all those kids was difficult, and on those days my grandfather *did* work, the money for food most often helped feed the children of the owner of the local beer garden instead. My mother was sent out to beg, but it still was never enough. Besides stone soup, the family ate a lot of *halushkies* and fried onions—cheap and delicious.

A proud member of SOMOS (and mother of novelist Summer Wood), Ellen Wood is an award-winning author, columnist and speaker. Her column, "Tips to Grow Younger," appears regularly in *The Taos News*.

Between a pinch and a teaspoon of salt
Between 3/4 cup and 1 cup of water
Between a cup and 1-1/2 cups of white flour
Maybe an egg
2 medium onions or one big one, chopped

Boil a big pot of water. In a big bowl, mix white flour and water. Start with a cup of flour and 3/4 cup of water. Mix with a fork. Add more water a little at a time and keep mixing. If too leaky, add more flour. Add salt. I have no idea how much. Just guess. If you're rich, add an egg.

Drop some of the dough from a spoon back into the bowl. If it slides easily off the spoon, it needs more flour. If it stays on the spoon and doesn't want to drop, it needs more water. It's ready when it placidly falls off, and then sort of springs back.

Put a colander in the sink. Wet a spoon in the boiling water, and then spoon out the *halushky* mixture into the water. You'll know the consistency isn't right if the mixture falls apart and disperses in the water—or if it clunks down to the bottom like a rock. It's just right if the *haluskies* float on top and keep their shape.

Don't dawdle. When you're all finished spooning the *halushky* mixture, in less than a minute they're done. Drain the *halushkies* into the colander.

Fry the onions in a big frying pan. When they're limp, throw in the *halushkies* and turn up the heat to brown everything. Salt and pepper them. Makes 2 to 4 servings.

Pasta Plates

Elvira's Quick marinara sauce

olive oil
fresh basil
3-4 cloves garlic, peeled,
           sliced
small can tomato paste
large can diced tomatoes
       or puréed or sauce

heat olive oil, sauté garlic
add basil leaves, add tomatoes.
  rinse cans with a little water
add put on simmer, partially cover
  pot (leave an opening) cover
    simmer for about an hour

cook pasta al dente
  drain, toss with sauce
    sprinkle with grated
      romano

113

GIOVANNA PAPONETTI

New Year's Eve Lasagna

In 1971 I moved to Shaftsbury, Vermont, from Connecticut. My parents were thrilled that I had found this vacation home for them. When they retired several years later, they moved there permanently and lived very fulfilling lives. The chalet was high on a hill with beautiful views. My young son and I would walk to a local farm to buy raw milk, or visit friends who owned an Arabian horse farm.

My family and friends were excited to visit me, so I invited them over for lasagna (made from a recipe passed down from relatives in Italy) to celebrate New Year's Eve on December 31, 1971. Wonderful smells permeated my home. I knew the lasagna was done when the cheese started bubbling. Everyone ate seconds and drank lots of red wine. After cleaning up in the kitchen, I returned to find my guests passed out. We missed New Year's Eve.

Giovanna Paponetti, author of *Kateri, Native American Saint,* is a muralist, painter and adjunct professor at UNM-Taos. She enjoys attending SOMOS events.

CLASSIC LASAGNA

1, 28-ounce can of crushed tomatoes

1, 8-ounce can tomato paste

1, 15-ounce can tomato puree

1, 15-ounce can stewed tomatoes

1 box of lasagna noodles

1 pound mozzarella cheese, thinly sliced

1 pound ricotta cheese

2 eggs beaten

Grated Parmesan cheese

1/4 cup parsley (for ricotta mixture)

1 tablespoon dried basil

1 tablespoon dried oregano

1 bay leaf

3 cloves of garlic, crushed

Salt and pepper to taste

1 pound lean ground beef

3 Italian hot sausages

Cook tomato sauce ingredients in crock pot overnight on low, or simmer in pot on stove for about 3 hours. Add small can of water. Preheat oven 350 degrees. Add eggs, salt, parsley to ricotta; set aside. Sauté whole sausages and meat in oil; set aside. Boil water, add lasagna noodles one at a time; cook 10 minutes. Drain pasta in colander. Return lasagna noodles to pot, tossing with a little oil to keep from sticking. Cut sausage in small pieces, and add with meat to sauce. Put thin layer of sauce on bottom of pan approximately 10 x 14 x 3-inches. Add 3 pieces of lasagna side by side. Spoon on layer of ricotta mixture then mozzarella. Add small amount of sauce on top. Repeat for five layers. Sprinkle top with grated cheese. Bake in oven. Cook until cheese bubbles, about one hour. Allow lasagna to cool slightly before cutting. Makes 8 servings.

Spaghetti Carbonara

During our first year in Florence in 1957, I made an unexpected friend: Elda, who had come to us as a maid and cook. Young, beautiful and buxom, with smiling brown eyes and wavy black hair, she welcomed me into our kitchen—now her domain.

We talked constantly as she worked, chopping and slicing and grating, her husky voice sharing stories of her young life. As the sun streamed through the kitchen windows, she performed magic before my eyes: thick, green olive oil and ruby vinegar becoming perfect salad dressing; the slow drizzle of olive oil whisked into egg, bringing forth creamy, rich mayonnaise.

Her greatest gift to me was her spaghetti carbonara, a rich blending of pasta, egg, butter, bacon, and "*parmigiano*." It was a dish invented by coal miners, she explained, who had nothing, but were able to make this robust comfort food with simple, elemental ingredients.

Elda and I cooked this pasta dish together, and thus began my ongoing culinary journey. I prepared this when newly married at twenty, and I still make it today, often casting my mind back to this angel in our kitchen in the Florentine hills.

Mag Dimond, currently a jewelry designer, photographer, and hospice worker in San Francisco, used to live in Taos and teach creative writing at UNM. In her twelve years in Taos, she formed deep friendships with artists, writers, students and teachers, and of course with SOMOS.

4 eggs, beaten

1/2 stick sweet (unsalted) butter, cut into bits

1 pound bacon, cut into 1-inch pieces

3/4-1 cup grated Parmesan cheese

Salt and freshly ground pepper to taste

1 pound spaghetti

Cook the bacon in a skillet, draining off the fat a couple of times. Set aside.

Cook the pasta in a large (8-quart) pot of boiling water (to which you've added about 3 tablespoons of salt) until it is al dente (firm but not hard). Drain.

Toss steaming pasta in a large bowl with beaten eggs, cooked bacon, butter bits and grated Parmesan. Add salt and freshly ground pepper to taste. Serve with extra Parmesan on the side. Makes 4 servings.

PAUL CHRISTIE

Victor's Spaghetti

I used to live in Philadelphia, one of those old-time East Coast cities made up of many neighborhoods. I lived in an area called the Art Museum neighborhood because it abuts the Philadelphia Art Museum, perched majestically over the Schuykill River alongside Fairmount Park.

At the time, the Art Museum area was becoming gentrified, meaning investors and speculators with no ties to the neighborhood were moving in to make a buck. So there was no really identifiable ethnic community there, and thus no local ethnic cuisine—unless you count a shot and a beer, with peanuts.

One of the first friends I made there was Victor Cimino. He had grown up in one of the great ethnic neighborhoods of Philadelphia—South Philly—but had migrated north to the Art Museum. Over the years, as Victor and I became fast friends, we started having Sunday afternoon get-togethers at one of his South Philly buddies' homes. Victor's friend Junior was a musician, a bass player, who had played with the likes of Vic Damone and Al Martino. He was also an opera buff. Our Sunday get-togethers blended spaghetti, wine and opera.

Making and eating Victor's spaghetti now always brings back good memories for me of old friends, old times and good food.

Paul Christie, now in New Mexico, is a friend of SOMOS.

SOUTH PHILLY-STYLE SPAGHETTI

6 cloves garlic, sliced very thin

1 small can of tomato paste

2 large cans of diced tomatoes

4 tablespoons virgin olive oil

2 pounds spaghetti, such as DeCecco brand

4-5 leaves fresh basil, chopped

1 teaspoon dried oregano

2 bay leaves

1/2 pound freshly grated Parmesan cheese

In a large saucepan, sauté garlic in olive oil over medium heat. When the garlic turns a golden color, add tomato paste and work into the oil, adding a little water to make it easier to blend. When the mixture is smooth, add the diced tomatoes, bay leaves, oregano and fresh basil. Mix all ingredients well, cover and simmer for one hour, stirring occasionally. In a large pot bring 6 to 8 quarts of water to a boil. Add a punch of salt and spaghetti. Cook 11 to 12 minutes until al dente. Drain water and place spaghetti in a large bowl (drizzle with olive oil). Pour sauce into a serving bowl, and offer cheese in a separate bowl. Serve with freshly baked Italian or French bread and a good red wine. Makes 6 servings.

Lulu's Pasta Sauce

An Italian boyfriend once goaded that he would only share his sauce recipe with me if we were married. I totally understood and admired him for it. I wasn't about to share mine with him either. My sauce is too easy. Thus far it's the only pasta sauce my current Italian boyfriend gives a 10, and I would be mortified if we ran across it at some other cook's table. I wonder if my father's father was hesitant to share his secret back in 1953 when he taught my mom this ancestral recipe.

My mom, Lulu, was a dental assistant at Fort Rucker in Southern Alabama when dad sat in her chair. The blue-eyed Yankee Sicilian swept her off her Southern, cotton-picking feet, and before you knew it had her ensconced in his parent's Lawrence, Massachusetts, home while he became a Sargent in the Korean War. Lulu, 98 pounds, buck-toothed and with a thick Southern drawl, was taken under her father-in-law's wing and given a two-year cooking course.

Today, as I crush each canned tomato by hand, squirting juice everywhere, I remember the love in my mom's hands and trust that that same love is making my sauce equally amazing.

Tara Lupo has lived in Taos, on and off, for sixteen years and considers it her true home. She has a great appreciation and fondness for the place SOMOS holds in the community.

ITALIAN TOMATO PASTA SAUCE

2 tablespoons good olive oil

1 large yellow onion, diced

Half a bulb of garlic, peeled and chopped fine

1/4 teaspoon crushed red pepper flakes

1 tablespoon dried basil

1/2 teaspoon fennel seeds

Salt and pepper

1 small can tomato paste

1/2 cup rich red wine

2 large cans whole, peeled tomatoes

1 bay leaf

2 pinches sugar

1 bunch Italian parsley, chopped

1/2 cup freshly grated Parmesan or Romano cheese

Heat the oil in a large pot with a heavy bottom. Add onion and a couple of pinches of salt, stirring to coat. Cook onions slowly, until translucent. Add the garlic and stir until the garlic releases its scent and mingles well with the onion. Add fennel, pepper flakes, basil, freshly ground pepper and a little more salt; stir for a minute or two. Add tomato paste, stirring until the tomato roasts a bit. Splash in the red wine and stir until well mixed and heated through. Add canned tomatoes, crushing them in your hands over the pot. Stir. Clean out all cans with warm water and add to the pot, along with another large can-full of water. Add bay leaf, sugar and parsley, stir well, and bring to a boil. Turn down the heat and adjust until you get the perfect simmer. Stir every 30 minutes or so. After 3 hours, stir in the grated cheese. The last hour of simmering needs to be watched more closely as the sauce is thicker and in danger of burning. Makes 4 servings.

KAYCE VERDE

Pesto Festival

My parents-in-law took to retirement by creating a mini-home-stead, complete with vegetable and flower gardens. There was always a bumper crop of basil, which couldn't go to waste. My mother-in-law took me under her wing when it was time to harvest the plants and turn them into pesto.

Every spring we packed up our cars and headed to Pawleys Island, just north of Charleston, South Carolina. The five-hour trip was made shorter by the honeysuckle intoxication. One year we invited friends for drinks and hors d'oeuvres, and they stayed into the dinner hour. Without a second thought, my in-laws jumped into action, taking out the pesto they had brought with them (kept frozen in ice cube trays), and, *voila*, the Annual Pesto Festival was born.

Our gathering was made even more special by our hunkered-down, funky cottage, which had survived a multitude of hurricanes. Just outside its old paned windows, we dined on benches around the long wooden table to the soothing sound of Atlantic waves.

SOMOS afforded poet Kayce Verde her first public reading in 1998, and she has been a member ever since. Her poetry has been published in *Chokecherries*, *The Practice of Peace*, *Earthships: The New Mecca Poetry Collection*, and *Sin Fronteras, Writers Without Borders*.

PESTO SAUCE

4 ounces fresh basil leaves (preferably home grown),
washed and patted dry
1/2 cup extra virgin olive oil
1/3 cup toasted pine nuts
1/2 cup Parmesan cheese
3-4 garlic cloves, peeled
Linguine pasta (enough for 8 servings)
Salt and freshly ground pepper

In a food processor fitted with a metal blade, chop the garlic cloves; add a few basil leaves and drizzle in the olive oil with the motor running. Keep adding the basil and olive oil until all are gone. Add the pine nuts and Parmesan and blend well.

Cook linguine according to directions; drain in a colander, leaving a little of the pasta water in the pot. Return the linguine to the pasta pot, add the pesto, and toss together.

Serve on warmed plates and sprinkle with a generous amount of grated Parmesan and toasted pine nuts. Makes 8 servings.

ROBERT J. SILVER

Extraordinary Ordinary Pasta

At anchor in an isolated island cove, we are transfixed by the slowly setting sun's radiating golden glow. A lone couple in love, it is our final night piloting a 35-foot sloop in subtropical, island-dotted, crystalline Caribbean waters.

Now at journey's end, provisions nearly exhausted, mere bits and pieces remain of the stores that initially overflowed every spare inch of the small boat's stowage space. Only assorted food fragments linger in our once crammed larder. Could a final feast be cobbled together from among these dregs, the not-yet-rotten residue of our desperately depleted stores?

Context and imagination dominate and propel. Assembled mundane ingredients are magically transformed. Treasured morsels of the improvised creation are savored as if gifts of the gods. Sun- and sea-addled, we declare this feast, composed of ordinary ingredients, to be among the best meals we'd ever consumed, a fitting finale to a soul-satisfying sail in paradise.

Robert J. Silver, an active member of SOMOS, practices forensic psychology and is a regular contributor to the Op-Ed pages of *The Taos News*. His creative nonfiction writing has appeared in *HOWL* and in *Chokecherries*.

Dried pasta (whatever you have), enough for two hungry vacationers
Several garlic cloves, peeled and forced through a garlic press
1/2 teaspoon hot red pepper flakes
1 teaspoon salt
1/3 cup extra virgin olive oil
1 can whole tomatoes in juice (preferably an Italian brand)
1/2 cup martini olives
Pinch of sugar (optional)
3/4 cup coarsely chopped fresh herbs, such as basil or parsley, or both

Cook pasta in a large pot of boiling salted water until al dente. While pasta boils, cook garlic, red pepper flakes, 1 teaspoon of salt and 1/2 teaspoon pepper in olive oil in a 12-inch heavy skillet over medium-high heat, stirring occasionally, until fragrant and pale golden, about 2 minutes. Meanwhile, coarsely chop the tomatoes, reserving their juice. Add chopped tomatoes to the pan, along with the olives, and some of the reserved juice, and simmer, stirring occasionally, until pasta is ready. Add a pinch of sugar, if desired. Drain pasta and add to sauce. Simmer, turning with tongs, until pasta is well coated. Makes 2 servings.

CHERIE BURNS

Skillet Macaroni

After I finished college in 1973 and started work in Denver, I moved into a three-bedroom apartment with two guys. They were older than I and had been working for several years, so they gave me a break on the rent. In return, I agreed to cook several nights a week.

I only knew a few of my Hoosier mother's down-home recipes, and my favorite was the easiest to make, skillet macaroni. I made a big cast iron skillet full. It seemed enough for an army. The next night I served it again, and the third night, too.

My roommates soon tired of skillet macaroni, and they've teased me about it now for forty years. One of them married a friend of mine, and we get together several times a year. I make skillet macaroni for their arrival at my house. When I visit them in Colorado or St. Louis and ask what I can bring, they always say, "skillet macaroni!" We get a laugh out of it.

My husband likes skillet macaroni, but not as much as my old friends do.

Cherie Burns is the author of three nonfiction books, the most recent of which is *Searching for Beauty: The Life of Millicent Rogers* (St. Martin's Press, 2011). She lives in Taos and is a board member of SOMOS.

1, 16-ounce box elbow macaroni (2 cups dry)

1 tablespoon vegetable oil

1 small onion, chopped

1 pound ground beef

1 pound Colby cheese, sliced

1, 28-ounce can Italian plum tomatoes

6 slices bacon

Salt, freshly ground pepper, and Tabasco sauce to taste

Cook the macaroni in a large pot of salted water according to the package instructions. Meanwhile, in a 10- to 12-inch black cast iron skillet, brown the onion in the oil; add the ground beef and cook, breaking it up with a fork to keep the chunks small. (If the meat is especially fatty, drain the fat off.)

Drain the cooked macaroni and add it to the skillet. Drain the canned tomatoes (saving the juice), crush them with your hand, and add them to the meat mixture, along with about a half-cup of the canned tomato juice. Salt and pepper generously and give a few shakes of Tabasco.

Cover the top with the cheese and bacon slices. (You might want to par-cook the bacon a bit beforehand.) Bake uncovered in a preheated 350-degree oven for about 40 minutes, until cheese has melted and the top appears golden brown. Makes 6 hearty servings.

Under the Hood

Chutn...
Thick white o...
Chicken Stock Cube
Orange juice
Apricot jom ± 2 tblsps
...over raw chicken
pieces pop in oven 200
Potatoes

Thick white onion soup
Butter
Bake in oven 200°
1 hr depending
on potatoes

Parolek
GARAGE
&
MACHINE SHOP

127

Manifold Delicacies

Over the years, as a manufacturer's representative, traveling salesman and truck driver, I've often cooked meals on the road. That is, I've used a camp stove or a campfire to cook what I like to eat. I've even had microwave ovens and hotplates in some of the trucks I've driven.

But I've since read about old-timers who cooked meals on their exhaust manifolds. In fact, the late, great Southwest anarchist writer Edward Abbey wrote about baking potatoes under the hood.

So I did some experimenting, and came up with some recipes and cookware solutions for those on the road and so inclined. I've even made wire baskets and loops to suspend the food over the exhaust manifold. This method works fine. But lately I've been using a loaf pan, which happens to fit perfectly in my car, a 1993 Mercury Tracer.

Cooking time is the biggest variable, so I've consolidated some of my research into the following list.

Peter Lewis learned to cook, read and write from his late mother who lived near Taos. He happened upon SOMOS while on a visit. He now writes Westerns and science-fiction books.

Buffalo Burgers:

Shape ground buffalo meat into patties. Wrap patties in aluminum foil; cook under the hood 50 minutes for well-done, 45 for medium, and 40 for rare.

Baked Potatoes:

Poke holes in spuds with a fork or knife; wrap in aluminum foil and bake under the hood for 2 hours.

Chile Con Carne:

Just lay a vented can in there, and your chile will be piping hot in 10 minutes.

Bread:

Mix and knead dough as you normally would; place in loaf pan and cover with aluminum foil. Bake in your under-the-hood oven for about 1 hour.

(Editor's note: In a recent "Click and Clack" column, the car guys Ray and Tom Magliozzi wrote about using a car's engine for cooking. "Since the car's exhaust manifold typically heats up to 800 degrees," wrote Tom, "there's more than enough heat in the engine compartment to cook anything you want." They even recommended a book on the subject: *Manifold Destiny*, by Chris Maynard and Bill Scheller.)

Breads & Biscuits

Banana Cake

2 cups flour
2 tspoons Baking Powder
1 tspoon Baking Soda

In a Blender
2 or 3 bananas
3/4 cup oil
1 cup sour cream
1 egg brown
1 cup
1 tp cinamon
1 cup wal
1 cup d

Christmas's Christmas Brioche

I owe a debt of gratitude to Betty Van Der Els, who forty years ago gave me the book *Homemade Bread* by the Food Editors of *Farm Journal*, along with strong encouragement that I could learn to make bread all by myself just by following its instructions. Betty suggested that I start with the simplest method she knew, the "CoolRise" recipes. Brioche became a family favorite for Christmas morning breakfast. I prepared the dough on Christmas Eve, let it rise in the refrigerator overnight, and popped it in the oven the next morning.

I gradually expanded my repertoire and became a self-taught baker, wildly popular with my four children and neighbors in Vermont. During the winter months, or about half the year, we heated with a wood stove, and the room where the stove was located made a perfect place for dough to rise. Our kitchen stove had two ovens, so I could bake eight to ten loaves at a time. I intensely enjoyed the process, especially the kneading and the eating.

I eventually became confident enough to teach an evening bread baking class at the University of Vermont called "Bread Baking for Health & Exercise." The exercise part was making eight loaves at a time.

Bill Christmas is a retired physician who has lived in Taos for the past eight years. He is married to Polly Raye, who enjoys his bread. They both applaud and support SOMOS.

CHRISTMAS BRIOCHE

6-7 cups of all-purpose flour
2 packages active dry yeast
1/2 cup sugar
1-1/2 teaspoons salt
1/2 cup softened butter
1-1/3 cups hot tap water
4 eggs at room temperature
1 egg yolk
1 tablespoon milk

Combine 2 cups flour, undissolved yeast, sugar and salt in a large bowl. Add softened butter. Add hot tap water to ingredients in bowl all at once. Beat with electric mixer at medium speed 2 minutes, scraping bowl occasionally. Add the 4 eggs and 1-1/2 cups more flour. Beat with electric mixer at high for 1 minute, or until thick and elastic. Gradually work in just enough of the remaining flour to make a soft dough. Turn dough onto a floured surface and knead for 5 to 10 minutes. Cover and let rest 20 minutes. Punch down and divide dough into unequal portions of 1/4 and 3/4. Roll out each portion and cut into 25 to 30 pieces each. Form each piece into a ball by rolling between your palms. Place a large ball in a muffin pan or cup, indent the top, and press a small ball into the indentation. Cover loosely with plastic wrap and place in the refrigerator for 2 to 24 hours. When ready to bake, remove plastic wrap and let stand at room temperature for 10 minutes. Bake at 350 degrees for 15 minutes, remove from oven and brush with egg yolk/milk combination. Return to oven for 5 to 10 minutes longer or until golden. Remove from pans immediately and cool on racks. Serve with jam or honey. Makes 25 to 30 rolls.

JAN M. SMITH

Anadama Bread

"Anna, damn you!" My father's stern voice soared above the other eight family members at the dinner table. He lamented the burnt roasts, mushy vegetables and bland side dishes my mother, Anna, prepared. Unlike her, my father was a wonderful cook, but he reserved his talents for special holidays. That didn't stop him from criticizing her daily fare.

On rare occasions he'd make one of our favorites, Anadama Bread. This is a traditional New England bread made with corn meal, molasses and white flour. One popular myth of its origins hails from the fishing village of Rockport, Massachusetts, in the 1880s: A fisherman, angry with his wife Anna for serving him nothing but cornmeal and molasses, one day adds flour and yeast to his porridge and eats the resultant bread, while cursing, "Anna, damn her!"

Years later, when all of us kids were grown, my father started a family tradition of baking a loaf of Anadama Bread for each of us at Christmas. Even though he died many years ago, one of us in the family always makes a baker's dozen of loaves of Anadama Bread every year.

That's how this recipe went from being a curse to a blessing in our lives.

Jan Smith has been the curator for the SOMOS Winter/Summer Writers' Series since 2009. She is an MFA candidate in Creative Writing at Goddard College.

2/3 cup yellow corn meal, plus 1 tablespoon for sprinkling

1 tablespoon salt, plus 1/2 teaspoon for sprinkling

1/2 cup molasses

3 tablespoons shortening

2 packages active dry yeast

6-7 cups all-purpose flour

Butter for greasing pan

Cook corn meal in 2-1/2 cups water and salt in a saucepan until thick, stirring with a wooden spoon. Put cooked cornmeal into mixer; add shortening and molasses and mix to blend. Allow this mixture to cool to lukewarm. Soak yeast in 1/2 cup lukewarm water. When the cornmeal mixture is lukewarm, add yeast and gradually mix in flour on the lowest speed to form a stiff dough. Cover and let rise in a warm place for one hour. Form into 2 loaves; put in greased bread pans (9 x 5 x 3-inch size). Brush with melted butter. Mix 1 tablespoon cornmeal with 1/2 teaspoon salt. Sprinkle over loaves. Cover and let rise another hour. Bake 15 minutes in a 400-degree oven, then 35 to 45 minutes at 350 degrees. Makes 2 loaves.

Zucchini Applesauce Bread

It wasn't exactly the first home I had imagined. Newly married in 2002, Jacob and I climbed the rickety steps to the trailer home in Burns, Oregon, that we would live in for the summer. As we peeked through the front door, I was definitely wary of being carried over this particular threshold.

The house had obviously not been occupied for some time. Cobwebs lurked everywhere, and a layer of grime covered the floor. There was clear evidence of mice and rumors of frogs in the shower. What kind of house had I gotten myself into?

Jacob and I went to work, scrubbing and scouring a semblance of a comfortable home for ourselves. Then one afternoon, after receiving some extra zucchini from a neighbor, we decided to bake bread. Unfortunately, our oven didn't work. Undaunted, we pulled out our Dutch oven.

After borrowing various ingredients from another friend and figuring the right amount of coals to heat the oven, we smelled the welcome aroma of fresh bread. That zucchini bread was the most delicious I've ever tasted, and I was happy to share it, realizing that wherever I was, as long as I had my family and kind friends around me, I could always find a home.

Morgan Young moved to Taos with her young family five years ago. She was first introduced to SOMOS by attending the Taos Storytelling Festival and has looked forward to it every year since. She thanks her mother-in-law, Shawnee Young, for this recipe.

3 eggs

1/2 cup vegetable oil (such as canola)

1/2 cup applesauce

2 cups sugar

2 cups grated zucchini (unpeeled)

3 cups all-purpose flour

1 tablespoon vanilla

1 teaspoon salt

1 teaspoon baking soda

1/2 teaspoon baking powder

1 teaspoon ground cinnamon

A dash of nutmeg

1 cup chocolate chips (optional)

1 cup chopped nuts (optional)

Preheat oven to 350 degrees. Grease two loaf pans. In a large bowl, mix all of the ingredients, adding the zucchini last. Pour into loaf pans and bake for one hour.

(Morgan's note: To cook bread in a 12-inch Dutch oven, you'll need 24 to 25 coals. Place one-third of the coals in a circle under the oven, and spread the remaining two-thirds evenly over the top. Bake for one hour.)

RACHEL MERCER

Summer Days Cornbread

As kids, my best friend Sierra and I were early entrepreneurs. We started a company called R 'n' S, which revolved around a red wagon packed with wares of our own creation: a thermos full of acorn tea, made from acorns bobbing in hot water; greeting cards artfully hand-drawn; jars of our famous Jum-Jum Jam, made from only the freshest of mashed up fruits from the refrigerator. On hot summer days we peddled our wares up and down the dirt roads on which we lived, calling out in reedy voices, "R and S! Get it fresh!"

Our true specialty was cornbread muffins. As seven- or eight- year-olds, we impressed ourselves by undertaking the complex process of baking—mixing the correct ingredients, pre-heating the oven (always hard to remember), waiting and waiting for the timer to buzz, and then the pure satisfaction of breaking open a real live muffin that we alone had worked to create. While the Jum-Jum Jam and sage bundles, tied messily with twine, were nodded over by the adults on whose doors we knocked and who humored us for several minutes, the muffins were a huge success.

Rachel Mercer, a friend of SOMOS, grew up in Taos in the nineties. She loves baking, especially pies—peach in summer and pear in winter. She also loves writing and wishes there were a recipe for that as well.

CORNBREAD

1 cup all-purpose flour

1 cup cornmeal

1/2 teaspoon salt

3 tablespoons sugar or honey

2 teaspoons baking powder

1 teaspoon baking soda

1 egg

1 cup buttermilk

3 tablespoons butter (plus a little to grease the pan)

Preheat oven to 350 degrees. Butter a large cast iron skillet. Melt the 3 tablespoons of butter in a small saucepan and set aside. Combine the dry ingredients in a large mixing bowl. In a separate bowl, stir together the egg and the buttermilk and add the melted butter. Pour the wet ingredients into dry and mix until just combined. Don't over-mix. Pour the batter into the skillet, smoothing out the edges with a spatula. Bake for 20 minutes until the top is golden brown, or until a toothpick inserted into the middle of the cornbread comes out clean. This cornbread can also be made into individual muffins using a muffin tin. Makes 12 servings.

VICKIE FORD

Flour Sack Biscuits, the Modern Way

My mother and father married in September of 1929. Dad was a range rider cowboy, and Mom was a recent high school graduate. Her skills included knitting, sewing, and cooking on a large wood-burning range. In October, the newlyweds headed to "cow-camp" to round up the cattle before winter. One of the perks at cow-camp was a one-room, dirt-floored cabin located in the high country, miles from town. The cabin's tiny wood-burning stove was large enough to cook a few things, plus heat the cabin.

My father had learned to mix his version of biscuits in the top of a 50-pound flour sack. Cowboys have no mixing bowls. Dad instructed Mom in this skill, so one evening while he was attending to chores outside, she gave the flour sack biscuits a try. The finished products resembled hardtack and were not edible.

Jokingly, Dad decided to tack a biscuit above the door. He announced that until she "got it right" he would advertise Mom's failure with another biscuit nailed above the door. Mom reported that she "had quite a line of biscuits" nailed over the door before she finally got it right.

Vickie Ford grew up in Colorado, not far from where this recipe was devised. A Taos resident since 2006, she enjoys playing the piano, cooking, and writing. Vickie's friends on the SOMOS board asked her to submit this entry.

2 cups all-purpose flour

1 teaspoon salt

1 teaspoon baking powder

2 teaspoons granulated sugar

3/4 to 1 cup heavy cream

1/4 cup melted butter, for dipping biscuits

Sift the dry ingredients together and fold in the heavy cream until it makes a soft dough that can be easily handled. Knead dough on a floured board for about 1 minute. Pat to a thickness of 3/4 inch. Cut in rounds or squares, dip in melted butter, and arrange in a greased square baking pan. Bake in a preheated 425-degree oven for 15 to 18 minutes until browned on top and cooked through. Makes 4 servings.

PATRICIA K. TOLLISON

Nanny Perry's Cheese Biscuits

Picture an elegant, silver-haired lady, well into her eighties, who, unlike many of her peers, still loved to cook. Nanny Perry was our downstairs neighbor in Charlottesville, Virginia, more than forty years ago. I actually never knew her given name. She introduced herself as "Nanny Perry" and that's what we called her. The yummy smells from her kitchen made the walk up our back stairs a daily pleasure, and we were fortunate to be frequent recipients of her artistry. A tin of anything from her oven was a treasured gift.

I was not yet truly proficient at boiling eggs, but Nanny Perry taught me how to make her cheese biscuits. We were neighbors for less than a year, but through this recipe, she has never left our lives. These tasty nibbles have continued as a family tradition and as holiday gifts for friends and neighbors all these years. It really isn't Christmas until I've made a double recipe and filled numerous tins. Now my daughter-in-law has started her own tradition of making Nanny Perry's cheese biscuits. They are perfect with a salad, at the cocktail hour, or really any time you feel like smiling.

Patricia K. Tollison is a psychologist and writer living in Austin, Texas. She loves Taos and SOMOS.

CHEESE BISCUITS

1/2 pound New York extra sharp cheddar, grated
1/2 pound unsalted butter, at room temperature
3/4 teaspoon salt
1/4 teaspoon red pepper, or to taste
Dash of Tabasco sauce, or to taste
2 cups all-purpose flour
1 cup ground pecans

Cream the cheese, butter, salt, red pepper, and Tabasco together by hand. (You can do this in a food processor, but I never have.) Work in the flour and pecans a bit at a time until the sides of the bowl are clean. Either drop by teaspoonfuls on greased cookie sheet or roll out on floured surface and cut as biscuits. Bake at 350 degrees for 15 minutes, adjusting for your oven and how thinly you rolled them out. Let cool and store in a tin. Makes at least 3 dozen biscuits.

Sauces, Salsas, Dips, Jams & Nibbles

Plum Jam

2 lbs Italian purple plums, washed
1 c. sugar

Halve plums and place, w/ pits + sugar,
in large Pyrex. Microwave on
covered, 15 min. Uncover,
stir well, + microwave, uncovered,
5-10 min. Strain through sieve;
discard skin + pits + reduce (on High)
to 16 oz (2 cups). Store in lidded
jar in fridge.

Strawberry - Rhubarb Jam

Wash, hull fresh, sweet strawb...
Place in large Pyrex bowl w/...
washed, sliced fresh rhubarb...
Cover + microwave on High...
10-15 min, until cooked + thick...
(See Rhubarb)

147

Honey Boy BBQ Sauce

Jason Goodhue, the proprietor of Taos Valley Honey, is best known in these parts as "Honey Boy." Jason and I have been over the road together, literally, walking the Camino de Santiago de Campostela with Taos's version of Sancho Panza, Andy Garcia; but that is another story.

Raised on generic Sue Bee, my first real education in honey began with a jar or two of Jason's latest harvest left on my doorstep. I then graduated into an amassed fortune in the best prize-winning honey in New Mexico: tiny heirloom jars sealed in beeswax; a rare water white whipped with raspberries; a filtered towhead from the San Luis Valley good for glazing tarts; a dark, syrupy amber, tasting of the gathered essences of clover, asters, sunflowers—a honey so complex in flavor that I was immediately convinced that honey could be as nuanced as wine.

Over the years Jason and Andy not only accompanied me over the Pyrenees, they also taught me the art of barbecue. I use Jason's dark amber honey in this barbecue sauce for pork spareribs, grilled for three hours over black oak coals.

Lise Goett is a poet who has taught benefit workshops for SOMOS. Her work has won numerous awards, including the 2012 Robert H. Winner Memorial Award from the Poetry Society of America.

148

HONEY BARBECUE SAUCE

1-1/2 cups chopped yellow onion (1 large onion)

1 tablespoon minced garlic (3 cloves)

1/2 cup vegetable oil

10 ounces tomato paste

1 cup cider vinegar

1 cup honey, preferably Taos Valley Honey amber

1/2 cup Worcestershire sauce

1 cup Dijon mustard

1/2 cup soy sauce

1 cup hoisin sauce

2 tablespoons chile powder

1 tablespoon ground cumin

1/2 tablespoon crushed red pepper flakes

In a large saucepan on low heat, sauté the onions and garlic with the vegetable oil for 10 to 15 minutes, until the onions are translucent but not browned. Add the tomato paste, vinegar, honey, Worcestershire sauce, mustard, soy sauce, hoisin sauce, chile powder, cumin, and red pepper flakes. Simmer uncovered on low heat for 30 minutes. Use immediately or store in the refrigerator. Makes 1-1/2 quarts.

KATHY FITZGERALD

Mango Salsa

I had my first mango the summer before I entered college in 1969. I was spending too much time stuck with my mother in a remote, rustic beach house on the island of Martha's Vineyard, pining for a boyfriend who lived across the Atlantic, and wishing I could escape to Woodstock. Each languid day was indistinguishable from the next that endless summer.

One day my mother brought home several mangoes. I'd seen mangoes in gourmet supermarkets, but I'd never tasted one. I slumped about in my bikini watching her as she fastidiously sliced a mango into delicate slivers for the luncheon guests. When she started in on the next one, something about that bursting, glistening, orange flesh and its exotic aroma set me off—or maybe it was teenage hormones kicking in.

As if possessed, I snatched the mango off the table, skipped out the door, ripping the fruit apart with my teeth, sucking in its juices, which dripped all over my face and neck as I ran to the seashore, moaning with pleasure at each bite. I devoured every shred of pulp off the oval pit, then rubbed the softly rounded pit all over my scantily clad body as if it were a bar of soap and I desperately needed a bath. Then I plunged into the crashing surf...

Since that day I've eaten mangoes countless times in every way, shape and form. But there was only one "first time," that summer of '69.

Kathy Fitzgerald, who is on the SOMOS board, prepares salads and veggies for her family, while her husband cooks the meat and pasta.

1/2 pineapple, peeled and cut into small chunks

1 red onion, peeled and diced

1/4 cup rice vinegar

1 teaspoon ground cumin (or more, to taste)

A dash of habanero chile sauce

3 fresh, ripe mangoes, peeled and diced

Fresh cilantro for garnish

Combine all except the mangoes and cilantro in a bowl and allow to marinate at least 3 hours, refrigerated. Before serving, add the mangoes, stir well, and top with fresh cilantro. Makes 4 servings.

JOANNE NELSON

Bedtime Snacks

At night Mom and I would crawl into her bed with a bag of potato chips and a bowl of dip between us, the family dog at our feet, tail thumping, always hopeful. We ignored his entreaties and concentrated on our reading material; me with my *Little House* books, Mom with her magazines.

The radio played next to her, a talk show host's voice soothing and indistinct, just a hum in the background to me. Mom listened closely though, and looked up from her magazine when callers with familiar problems got through. She'd lift her hand as a "be quiet" signal if I crinkled the bag.

Now and then Dad peeked in to comment, "It's a damn library in here," or "When's she going to bed?" before shaking his head and walking away. But it wasn't a library because we had our bowl of creamy, oniony dip and that salty bag of chips on the blankets between us as we read.

One chip after another dipped into the bowl, sometimes our hands connecting when we reached at the same time, and occasionally Mom's wedding ring thunking against the side of the metal bowl, a harsh sound in the quiet room.

Joanne Nelson is a writer and psychotherapist living in Hartland, Wisconsin, with her family. She grew up in Milwaukee in the sixties. She considers herself a Midwestern link to SOMOS.

FRENCH ONION CHIP DIP

8 ounces of cream cheese
1 beef bouillon cube
1/2 envelope (about 1 tablespoon) Lipton Onion Soup Mix
1/8 teaspoon garlic powder

Dissolve beef bouillon cube in 4 ounces (1/2 cup) of hot water. In a medium bowl, combine the cream cheese, dry soup mix, and garlic powder. Add 3 tablespoons of the bouillon liquid. Beat well. Serve with potato chips, pretzels, or cut vegetables. Store in the refrigerator (if there are any leftovers). Makes 8 servings.

Taos Raspberry Jam

Anyone who tries to garden between Taos's late and early frosts knows the challenge. We need to trade strategies.

A friend had success with Heritage raspberries and gave me some plants. He warned against the temptation to let the old canes bear in the spring. Go for a one-crop season, he advised; cut the plants down in the fall so new canes get all the energy in spring.

I first planted my berries in partial sun with somewhat irregular irrigation and got vigorous brambles, lots of green berries, and a few rock-hard red ones before frost. That fall I cut down the bushes, shortened the length of my vegetable garden, and transplanted the dormant raspberries to my best soil and water system and most sun. I gained a buzzy bee haven and canes bent down with sweet berries.

It was time to make jam for myself, as well as gifts for others. It's not just jam you can share. Every fall the bushes have runners that need thinning. Friends now nurture these plants throughout Taos.

Linda Malm, a former college dean, is a NM Master Gardener and currently one of the Writers of Los Luceros (the Robert Redford/NM Film Board enterprise). Her poetry has appeared in a variety of magazines, anthologies, and several online publications. She has been a member of SOMOS for eight years.

RASPBERRY JAM

2 pounds ripe raspberries, unwashed (unless sprayed)
2 peeled shredded Granny Smith or other tart apples
3 cups granulated sugar
4-6 half-pint Ball jars that have been kept in hot water
after having been boiled for 17 minutes

Put the berries, apples and sugar in a heavy pot and, stirring constantly, bring to a rapid boil, continuing to boil until the liquid reaches the "soft ball" stage (207-209 degrees at 7,000 feet altitude). Skim foam. Pour into the sterile jars, leaving 1/4-inch space at the top. Loosely tighten the metal rings. Process by boiling the filled jars in water for 15 minutes. Remove the jars with tongs and allow to cool in a draft-free place at room temperature. You may hear popping sounds as the lid vacuums seal. After 12 hours, remove the rings and test the seals. The lid should curve down slightly and should not move when lightly pressed in the center. Tighten the rings.

Lee Lee's Apricot-Ginger Jam

In the valleys above and around Taos, ancient orchards continue to produce heirloom varieties of apricots and apples. A highlight for my young son Thatcher Gray was attending community gatherings around a goat roast and fruit harvest on Sabine Wilms's little farm in Talpa.

Being a violinist, Sabine would attract other stringed aficionados. On one occasion in 2010, her orchard was filled with the melodious musings of Mendelssohn played by a string quartet set in the soft green grass of early summer. It was as if the music infused the apricots with its sweet sounds as we climbed and shook and otherwise coaxed succulent jewels from their limbs. We left with huge baskets of delicate orange flesh, fingers sticky, bellies full, and minds wondering what to do with thirty pounds of apricots.

When the season rounded out and cool air crisped the apples, her goats would feast on fallen fruit. We would in turn enjoy the sweetness of their milk as we pulled down buckets of apples for our own consumption. Sabine always said it was in her German nature not to waste anything, and she would generously share her apples and instructions on how to put them up. Sabine has since moved to Oregon, and we miss her.

Lee Lee, a member of SOMOS, is a visual artist who is creating the *Tales of Thatcher Gray*, children's books that explore contemporary issues such as local food production (www.talesofthatchergray.com).

APRICOT-GINGER JAM

5 pounds firm but ripe fresh local apricots, quartered and pitted
4-1/2 cups of sugar
1/4 cup of peeled, chopped, fresh ginger
1 (1-3/4 ounce) box of powdered pectin
7 apricot kernels (or 1/2 teaspoon of almond extract)

In a large bowl, toss together the apricots, apricot kernels, ginger and 4 cups of the sugar. Refrigerate for 8 to 24 hours. Transfer apricot mixture to a large pot and bring to a boil. Boil for 20 minutes, stirring frequently. Reduce heat and simmer for 35 to 60 minutes more, stirring frequently as the jam thickens.

While the jam cooks, whisk together pectin and remaining 1/2 cup of sugar. When the jam is thick, add the pectin mixture. Return to a rolling boil, whisking constantly, for 1 minute. Fill sterilized jars, leaving 1/4-inch headspace. Seal the jars and process in a boiling water bath for 17 minutes (or 10 minutes at sea level). Makes about 8 half-pint jars.

MARTI STOCKER

The Cowboy Way

Didn't I sign up for this dude ranch vay-cay because my friend Jordan said it never rains out here in the summertime? Some fun. Where are those sunny days? I know: Wait fifteen minutes and the weather will change. No change in two days. I'm stuck in this God-forsaken place, and I can't even call my bff. Who woulda thought my cell would die?

CRASH!

What was that? Now the lights are flickering. I'm gonna be stuck in the dark soon. What did I get myself into?

The cabin door bursts open as Dan, the ranch owner, lunges in carrying a box of gourmet snacks.

"You scared me," I tell him. "But it's about time somebody came to rescue me."

"Did you miss me?" He smiles. "We might as well make the best of this storm. While I change out of these wet duds, you could pour us two glasses of wine. I've been saving this bottle of Pinot Grigio. You'll find plates and glasses in the cabinet."

He retreats quickly to the bedroom.

"Where did you get wine?"

"At the lodge," he calls out. "They passed out picnic meals. It might be a while before the electricity comes on. Let's make the best of your stay."

Dan returns wrapped in a Western-themed quilt. "Come warm me," he says. He opens the quilt to enfold me as we kiss and fall back onto the cordovan leather sofa in front of the fire.

"What am I gonna tell my bffs when I get back to the city and they ask, 'Did you have any fun?'"

"That you experienced some real Western hospitality, the cowboy way."

Marti Stocker, who lives in Denver, is a storyteller, a playwright, and a friend of SOMOS and Taos. She is currently researching and writing a play about Mabel Dodge Lujan.

SWEET AND SAVORY NUTS
(a Martha Stewart recipe)

1 large egg white
1 teaspoon cocoa powder
1 teaspoon ancho chile powder
1/2 teaspoon ground cinnamon
1/2 teaspoon sea salt
1/4 cup sugar
2 cups raw nuts (pecans, cashews, peanuts, walnuts, almonds,
pistachios, or macadamias)

Preheat oven to 325 degrees. Lightly beat egg white in a large bowl. Add dry ingredients; mix until slightly frothy. Fold in nuts. Oil a rimmed baking sheet. Pour mixture onto sheet, spreading nuts in a single layer. Bake until crispy, 40 to 45 minutes, turning once after 20 minutes. Cool completely before serving. Makes 2 cups.

ROBIN REESE

Sap Crunchers

After reading *Full Moon Feast: Food and the Hunger for Connection* by Jessica Prentice, I was hungering for some connection of my own. It was early March 2007, and the so-called Sap Moon was fast approaching. My first full-moon feast!

For the connection, I decided to use maple syrup as the "sap" in the following recipe. Nothing could be simpler. It's even become a sort of trademark for me. I created this for a dinner party at my house. I added the fragrant nuts to an otherwise simple green salad (although I've since discovered they perk up most anything, including steamed vegetables, grains and ice cream.) The maple syrup and pecan flavors are a delightful compliment. The little crunch adds interest to most foods.

At their party debut that evening, I asked my guests what I should call them. Without missing a beat, one of the men called out, "Sap Crunchers!" It stuck.

A former television producer and director, Robin Reese is a recent émigré to Taos from San Francisco. She says she looks forward to becoming more involved with SOMOS "on a myriad of levels."

PECAN CRUNCHERS

2 cups (about) pecan halves
3-4 tablespoons genuine maple syrup
Sea salt

Pour the pecan halves into an iron skillet. As the pan heats to medium, toss the toasting pecans every so often. (You don't want to burn them.) When you begin to smell the rich warm smell of pecans (about 10 minutes or so), pour a few tablespoons of maple syrup into the hot pan. (Be sure to use the real stuff, which should be kept in your refrigerator after opening.)

Turn off the heat. Continue tossing the nuts in the syrup. The goal is to coax the syrup to stick to the nuts and not the pan. Within minutes, when you feel enough of a connection has been made, dump the sticky nuts onto a cutting board or counter. Keep tossing. The idea is to keep the Crunchers from sticking together. They firm up as the syrup cools. Sprinkle with a bit of sea salt and store in the refrigerator. Sap Crunchers keep for months and make a nutritious travel snack.

Sweet Stuff

Brandy Tart.

1½ cups Flour, ¼ tsp. Baking Pow___
¼ tsp Salt, 1½ cups date___
___ ¼ cup butter, 1 tsp. Bicarb ___
water, 1 egg, 1 cup sugar.

Method

1. Mix dates, bicarb. w___
2. Cream butter and suga___
3. add egg.
4. add rest of ingred___
5. Bake at 300° Fah. ___

Sauce

2 cups sugar 1 cup ___
1. Boil together bu___ ___
2. add 1 tablespoon ___
___ and 1 cup of bran___

162

163

JUDITH KENDALL

Classic High-Altitude Cake

"Mom! What happened to the cake?!" was too often the cry from my son and daughter when the birthday cake I had so lovingly prepared was cut and served. Raised in New England, I was accustomed to creative doll, train, bear, and crazy cakes baked by my mom for every special occasion. We had star cakes at Christmas, strawberry shortcakes at the first sign of summer, and pumpkin cakes in the fall.

After my children were born, I naturally wanted to pass along this tradition. Alas, Taos's altitude presents a special challenge to any baker. Every cake I baked had a huge hole in the middle. In the oven it bubbled away and then sank deeply, no matter what adjustments I applied. I definitely covered the hole with yummy frosting, but usually there was more frosting than cake. Bear in mind, my children never protested all that sugar, and every cake was devoured.

Yet, I was miserable, explaining to them," If your grandmother made this it would be a tall, proud cake, sending you birthday love."

Recently, after admiring the cakes at Sugar Nymphs restaurant in nearby Penasco, I asked for the secret. The chef there presented to me her worn, greasy copy of Susan Purdy's *Pie in the Sky* cookbook, calling it her baking bible. Believe me, this recipe from *Pie in the Sky* works—even at Taos's 7,000 feet. Hooray for happy (and successful) birthday cakes!

Taos educator, gallery owner, friend of SOMOS since its inception and participator in the mentorship program for many years, Judith Kendall loves to cook for friends and family.

CLASSIC HIGH ALTITUDE CAKE

3 cups, plus 3 tablespoons all-purpose flour

2 teaspoons baking powder

3/4 teaspoon salt

1/2 pound (2 sticks) unsalted butter, at room temperature

2 cups minus 2 tablespoons sugar

5 large eggs at room temperature

2 teaspoons vanilla extract

1 teaspoon almond extract

1-1/2 cups buttermilk (no substitutions)

Preheat oven to 350 degrees. Place rack in the center of the oven. Mix together flour, sugar, salt, and baking powder. In a mixer, cream together butter and sugar, adding eggs a few at a time. Add dry ingredients, blending and alternating with buttermilk. Pour into greased cake pans. Bake layers 22 to 27 minutes; sheet cake 30 to 32 minutes. Cool for 10 minutes. Frost as desired. Makes 8 to 12 servings.

(Judy's note: The secret to this cake's success is measuring the ingredients precisely.)

Allegra's Carrot Cake

What happens when you allow yourself to imagine doing the impossible? Like putting a man on the moon? Or, if you're me, baking a cake from scratch?

I wrote a short film script about Neil Armstrong's neighbors on the day the kid next door walked on the moon. It's a story that celebrates breaking the bounds of possibility, and I was financing it in that spirit: basically, by telling friends and strangers the story and asking them to give me twenty bucks. Then it occurred to me I should provide something in return: auction items, have a raffle. And what better way to sell raffle tickets than at a bake sale?

The fact that I didn't know how to bake could not be allowed to be relevant. Lots of friends offered to help, but I knew I'd feel like a fraud if I let them do all the baking. I searched online for carrot cake recipes, and with ignorant certainty rejected anything that involved crushed pineapple. What nobody told me was that you don't have to grate the carrots by hand.

With more bake sales—and birthdays—my baking confidence grew. I changed proportions, even changed ingredients. My new mantra: Yes, you can!

Allegra Huston, a longtime fan of SOMOS, is the author of the memoir *Love Child* and the screenwriter/producer of the award-winning short film "Good Luck, Mr. Gorski."

CARROT CAKE

4 eggs

1-1/4 cups walnut oil (don't totally fill the last quarter cup)

1-1/2 cups sugar

2 generous teaspoons vanilla extract

2 cups all-purpose flour

1-1/2 teaspoons baking soda

1-1/2 teaspoons baking powder

1/2 teaspoon salt

2 teaspoons grated nutmeg (or cinnamon, or a combination)

1 pound carrots, peeled and grated (using a food processor fitted with grating blade)

1 cup chopped walnuts

Beat together eggs, oil, sugar, and vanilla. Sift in flour, baking soda, baking powder, salt, and nutmeg. Fold in carrots and walnuts. Bake for 40 minutes at 350 degrees in a greased and floured 9 x 13-inch baking tin. Check that a toothpick comes out clean. (This works at Taos's altitude of 7,000 feet.)

Frost with cream cheese frosting: Beat together 1,16-ounce package of cream cheese, 1 stick of unsalted butter (at room temperature), 1-1/2 cups confectioners' sugar, and 2 teaspoons vanilla. Slather generously over cooled cake. Decorate with more walnuts, if desired. Makes about 12 servings.

LOUISE FERRARO DERETCHIN

Leonard Ferraro's Italian Cheesecake

It is the late 1960s in my parents' third-floor walk-up in Brooklyn. I am a newlywed, aching to take traditions with me to my new home. I lean on the kitchen table watching my father prepare the cake to serve with Christmas dinner.

He taps an egg on the edge of the mixing bowl. His hair glistens grey against his olive skin. Using one hand, he snaps the cracked eggshell backwards, releasing its contents. A short-order cook, he works quickly; a quiet man, he works silently. Tap, snap, toss, and on to the next one.

In no time twelve eggs like yellow polka dots lay atop the white, creamy mound of ricotta. The thirteenth, the one I crack, meanders in free form among the perfect circles.

"You need to get the lumps out of the ricotta. Not all of them. You can leave some." These are the only instructions he gives.

As a child, I watched with fascination. As an adult, I watch to learn. I write down portions and quantities. He does not measure or count. The gentle smile on his lips betrays his pride as he mixes, pours, and bakes.

The only recipe of his I am able to replicate is this one for Italian cheesecake. Maybe it's because of the warmth I feel as I think of him while I am mixing, pouring, and baking. Or maybe he made the recipe simple enough that I would have no problem following it and remembering him.

Louise Ferraro Deretchin is an educator, writer and artist who divides her time between Taos, New Mexico, and The Woodlands, Texas. She is a member of SOMOS.

ITALIAN CHEESECAKE

2 pounds ricotta cheese
13 eggs
1-1/2 cups granulated sugar
2 tablespoons vanilla extract
Grated zest of 1 lemon
1/4 cup (2 ounces) mixed candied fruit
Confectioners' sugar

Preheat oven to 300 degrees. Grease and lightly flour a 9-inch spring form pan. Crack eggs into a large mixing bowl and beat them slightly. Force ricotta through a sieve to remove lumps. Add to the eggs. Add the sugar, vanilla, and lemon zest. Stir until well mixed. Stir in the candied fruit. Pour batter into prepared spring form pan. Bake about 2 hours or until light brown and slightly hard between the edge and half way to center. Cool and refrigerate until ready to use. (May be made two or three days in advance.) Sprinkle with confectioners' sugar just before serving. Makes 10 to 12 servings.

JUDITH NASSE

Summer Shortbread

I lugged the cutting board home from Pimlico on the 24 bus, then up the hill past Rumbold's Bakery, Keats' House, and on up the steep Hampstead Hill to my flat in London. It was probably 1972. The cutting board was solid wood, 2 inches thick, and weighed 9 pounds. It was a sunny day, so I was hot and tired by the time I got it into my tiny London kitchen. I am still proud of that purchase from Elizabeth David's cookery shop at 46 Bourne Street in Pimlico, London. I wish the shop were still there, as it was a mecca for me when I first taught myself to cook "proper" food, and it was were I learned of great quality cooking utensils and kitchenware.

I had grown up with typical American middle-class post-war fare, such as Mock Ravioli, fancy Jell-O salads with cottage cheese and macadamia nuts, and Campbell's Soup. I learned to cook young as the eldest of six children in California. I loved cooking. It was my first art form, really. Imagine my delight when I moved to London in 1968, when culture there was expanding with Mary Quant, the Beatles, Carnaby Street, and Elizabeth David as monarch of the movement to bring the best cuisine to England. I taught myself gourmet cooking from David's books and others. To this day my dog-eared, yellowed, falling-apart copy of Elizabeth David's *Summer Cooking* is still one of my favorites.

I'm fortunate to have lived in a few exotic places, such as London, Honolulu, and Taos, and to have visited many more, always collecting recipes. But I most often fall back on David's tried and true recipes. Here is one.

Judith Nasse is a SOMOS member and a Taos writer and artist. She is co-author of *Millicent Rogers: A Life in Full* (2012) with Art Bachrach and Nita Murphy.

RASPBERRY SHORTBREAD (OR CRUMBLE)

6 ounces flour (1-1/2 cups)

3-1/2 ounces (3/4 cup packed) moist brown sugar

2 ounces butter (4 tablespoons, or 1/4 cup)

1/2 teaspoon ground ginger

1 teaspoon baking powder

1 pound fresh raspberries (unwashed, unless sprayed)

A little white sugar

Put the raspberries in a fairly large, shallow pie dish, strew them with white sugar. Set aside. Cut the butter into very small pieces and crumble it with the flour until it is thoroughly blended. Add the brown sugar, ginger, and baking powder. Spread this mixture lightly over the raspberries, and smooth it out evenly, without pressing down. Bake in the center of a medium oven (350 degrees) for about 25 minutes. Serve hot or cold with a bit of thick cream poured over or with ice cream.
Makes 4 to 6 servings.

Shoo-Fly Pie

Growing up in the Pennsylvania Dutch (German) Country in the fifties, I enjoyed the many foods typical of the area, from potato filling and pepper cabbage to crumb pies. Shoo-Fly Pie was one of my favorite breakfast foods. Now people eat it as a dessert, and some like it with ice cream.

In the Amish homes there, one day of the week is set aside for baking. With so many breads, cakes and pies being made for the week, the kitchen gets very warm, so women open the kitchen windows and set the pies on the sill to cool. Quite naturally, flies are drawn to the pies' sugary topping.

Shoo-Fly Pie comes in four varieties: wet or dry bottom and dark or light, depending on how it is made. Wet or dry bottom refers to the layer just above the piecrust, which may be gooey-wet or cakey-dry. Dark or light depends on whether dark molasses or light Karo syrup is used. The following recipe is for a dark, wet-bottom pie.

JonnaLynn Mandelbaum has been a member of SOMOS since she moved to Taos twelve years ago. She is the author of three books on Mozambique. Her fourth book, on a different region, is in progress. For more, go to: http.tinyurl.caum/jonnalynn.

1, 9-inch unbaked pie shell

1-1/2 cups all-purpose flour

1/2 cup dark brown sugar

1 teaspoon cinnamon

1/2 teaspoon nutmeg

1/8 teaspoon ground cloves

1/4 teaspoon salt

1 stick (8 tablespoons) unsalted butter, cut up

1/2 cup molasses

1/4 cup corn syrup

1/2 cup water

1/2 teaspoon baking soda

In a medium bowl, mix flour, sugar, spices, salt, and butter into crumbs. In another bowl, combine the molasses, corn syrup, water, and baking soda. Pour liquid into pie shell. Carefully spoon crumbs over liquid. Bake on the bottom rack of a 400-degree oven for 20 to 30 minutes, or until crust is golden. Makes 6 to 8 servings.

Autumn Apple Pie

My memories of growing up in New England flood back every autumn....

The air is crisp, the leaves are turning shades of orange, brown and red, and there are signs of winter beginning to show their frosty presence.

My excitement is building as we all load up onto hay wagons with our baskets ready. As we trundle up and down the rows of trees, I can reach out and grab ripe and ready apples to munch on. There is nothing better than the taste of apples plucked right off the branches.

My sister and I choose the ideal tree. Joyfully, we scamper up and down ladders, loading our baskets and bellies with perfect apples. When we get home, my mother spends hours at her labor of love—peeling, slicing, and baking her apple pies. I love the aromas that fill our home. As we savor our slices of hot-from-the-oven pie, topped with cheddar cheese or vanilla ice cream, we know for certain that autumn has arrived.

Heather Leisher, a friend of SOMOS, is a mother living with her family in Taos. She loves reading and storytelling.

APPLE PIE (OR GALETTE)

1-1/2 cups all-purpose flour
8 tablespoons (1 stick) cold, unsalted butter, cut in dice
1/4 teaspoon salt
7-8 tablespoons ice-cold water
5-8 peeled, cored, and sliced cooking apples
1/4 cup sugar
1 teaspoon cinnamon
1/4 cup freshly squeezed lemon juice
3 tablespoons butter, cut into small pieces
Egg yolk
Confectioners' sugar

Work flour, 1 stick butter and salt together quickly with fingertips until well blended. Add ice water and, also quickly, work into dough (do not over-handle). Gather dough into a ball, cover and chill at least 30 minutes. On a floured surface, roll out the pastry into a large circle, about 1/4-inch thick. Transfer dough to a cookie sheet. Combine the apples, sugar, cinnamon, lemon juice, and remaining butter in a bowl and cover the center of the pastry with the filling mixture. Gently fold the edges of pastry up over the apples, leaving an opening in the middle. Brush the pastry with an egg wash (egg yolk mixed with 1 to 2 tablespoons of water). Bake for 45 to 60 minutes at 400 degrees, until golden. Cool slightly and dust with confectioners' sugar. Makes about 8 servings.

(Editor's note: This country-style pie, or free-form tart, is what the French call a galette.)

SUSAN ERLANDSON WASHBURN

Pavlova

I recently unearthed a faded photo of something resembling an enormous squashed marshmallow coated in whipped cream and embellished with sliced kiwifruit and raspberries. Labeled "My First Pav," the photo records a rite of passage: my transformation from ex-pat Yank to proper New Zealand housewife. Back in 1982 I married a Kiwi and swanned off to the Antipodes to go gold mining. While most of my time was spent in the bush—wet, dirty and exhausted—I also had to stage elaborate dinners for potential investors in our mining venture. So whipping up a Pavlova, a meringue-based dessert as temperamental as the prima ballerina for whom it was named, was a skill as integral to my survival as the ability to ford swift braided rivers without being swept into the Tasman Sea. I don't ford many rivers these days, but I do like to impress dinner guests with this spectacular dessert, a medley of contrasting tastes and textures.

Susan Washburn, a former SOMOS youth mentor, recently completed a nonfiction book, *My Horse, My Self: Life Lessons from Taos Horsewomen*. She is now at work on a dark and dirty autobiographical novel about her misadventures as a gold miner in New Zealand.

Meringue:

6 egg whites, at room temperature, in glass or metal bowl (not plastic)

1 cup white sugar, preferably superfine

1 tablespoon cornstarch

1/8 teaspoon cream of tartar

A pinch of salt

2 teaspoons white vinegar

1 teaspoon vanilla

Topping:

1 pint of whipping cream

1/4 cup powdered sugar

1 teaspoon vanilla

Fruit:

Sliced kiwis with raspberries or passion fruit pulp. Alternatively, sliced peaches with blueberries or strawberries with bananas

Preheat oven to 300 degrees. Line a baking sheet with parchment, draw a 9-inch circle on it. Combine sugar, cornstarch, cream of tartar and salt in small bowl. Beat egg whites until stiff but not dry. Add sugar mixture gradually to egg whites, beating after each addition until thick and glossy (do not overbeat!). Fold in vinegar and vanilla.

Spoon mixture onto center of parchment circle, smoothing outward into a mound with a slight depression in center. Bake one hour or until outside is crisp. Cool on wire rack. Remove meringue from parchment and place on platter. Whip cream in small bowl, adding sugar and vanilla. Spread on meringue. Top with fruit. Makes 8 servings.

L'Arancio Dolce, or Sweet Orange

I spent my junior year in high school abroad in Viterbo, Italy. From my first night, when I sat down at the table with people whom I couldn't understand, to my last, speaking heatedly about politics and American pop stars, I was always presented a full plate of some delicious dish. Orders to take more—"*Mangia! Mangia!*" and "*Dai! Forsa!*" (literally, Go! With force!)—were common at our table. Though my elderly host-mom Christina's homemade pastas and rich cakes were incredible, my favorite dish was her orange dessert. She simply called it "*l'arancio dolce,*" the sweet orange.

I have a specific memory of sitting around the table with my best friend from the States and my host-brother Francesco. His mom Christina presented a plate of hyper-perfectly sliced oranges for us. We two American girls were amazed by their intense flavor. I asked Christina (in my iffy Italian), "*Perche e il cibo italiano sempre meglio degli altri?*" (Why is Italian food better than the rest?). She looked up through her half broken and crooked glasses, then back at the oranges and said, "*Perche usiamo l'olio in tutto!*" (Because we use oil in everything!)

Leyton Cassidy, while a student at Moreno Valley High School in Angel Fire, New Mexico, spent her junior year abroad in Italy. She and her parents moved from Berkeley, California, to Taos six years ago. Leyton has been involved in SOMOS since participating in the youth mentorship program in the sixth grade.

Peel oranges (about one orange per person) and slice them horizontally, about a centimeter thick. Arrange them on a plate.

Pour good quality Italian olive oil, a little bit more than you think is needed, over the plate of slices. (Pour for about five seconds.)

Keep adding sugar until you think that it is too sweet (about a handful per each three oranges).

Mix with your bare hands, but not too hard, because the oranges must stay intact. Sprinkle a little more sugar on top. Serve chilled.

Garnish with strawberries, but only when they are in season—in keeping with the Italian spirit.

(Leyton's note: This recipe for sweet orange was delivered in the oral tradition by my host-mother Christina Bernini. No real measurements are required.)

CARMEN A. LIEURANCE

Rosanna's Biscochitos

Familia and *tradiciones*—these are my mother Rosanna's legacy. Her home in Taos was located on Camino de la Placita. She invited family and friends to join her in baking the traditional New Mexico cookie, which is served at family gatherings, weddings, parties, and especially during the Christmas holidays.

The tradition of baking for Christmas the day after Thanksgiving was perfect, allowing time for the cookies to be infused with the smell and taste of the anise seeds. The cookies were stored in airtight containers until they were served or given as holiday gifts.

Rosanna lived to be one hundred years and nine months old. Even though her vision was diminishing with age, she looked forward to having family, young and old, sit with her and together roll and cut the dough, shaping the biscochitos and enjoying them when baked. We were learning a tradition from an amazing woman.

Her legacy will live on in the lives of our children, who have shared this special day-after-Thanksgiving baking tradition together, instead of going to the modern "black Friday sales." May her legacy find a place in your life, too, as you prepare the dough, shape each cookie, bake and enjoy them as they come out of the oven.

Carmen Lieurance is a native Taoseña. She and her husband have been married for forty-eight years, and they have two adult children. She loves attending the SOMOS Storytelling Festivals.

BISCOCHITOS

2 cups lard
1-1/2 cups sugar
2 eggs
3 teaspoons baking powder
1 teaspoon salt
5 cups all-purpose flour
1 cup whole wheat flour
3 teaspoons anise seeds
1/3 cup orange juice or apple cider
A mixture of sugar and cinnamon for sprinkling

Preheat oven to 350 degrees. Cream together the lard, sugar, eggs, baking powder and salt. Alternately, add the flour and the liquid to the creamed mixture, until a soft (not sticky) dough is formed.

On a floured surface, roll out the dough to about 1/4-inch thickness. Cut into desired shapes. Sprinkle cookies with the cinnamon-sugar mixture. Bake at 350 degrees for 10 to 15 minutes, or until golden brown. Makes 5 dozen cookies.

Peanut Butter Cookies

"Daddy loves these kind of cookies, doesn't he mommy?"

"Yes, he does. We make them exactly like his grandma made them."

"More peanut butter, mommy?"

"Yes. You need to fill that measuring cup all the way up."

"Will you tell him when he comes home that I made them for him?"

"No, you can tell him yourself."

My mother nodded and smiled, the gap between her front teeth marked. "That's why you're doing all the work."

Her thin arm pushed against the rough dough. "It's hard to mix. Will you help me? ... Use your hands. It's okay. Go ahead. Good..."

Tiny fingers mashed and kneaded the goo.

"Now a spoonful for each one, then push them down with a fork. Like this.... See?" She threw back her head and giggled as she watched me. Then we sat at the window waiting for his white car to sidle up to the house.

"Daddy, daddy!" I grabbed his big brown hand and pulled him to the kitchen. "Look what I made for you! Are you hungry? I made them all by myself just for you! Mommy helped a little bit. Are they good? Are they just like your grandma's?"

Amber Gordon, a friend of SOMOS, is a Taos writer, mother, wife, and instructor.

1 cup creamy peanut butter

1-1/3 cups sugar

1 egg

1 teaspoon vanilla extract

1 teaspoon cinnamon

Preheat oven to 350 degrees. Grease a sheet pan. In a mixing bowl combine the peanut butter, sugar, egg, vanilla, and cinnamon then stir well with a spoon. Roll into balls half the size of golf balls. Place dough on the prepared baking sheet. With a fork dipped in water, press a crisscross design on each cookie. Bake for 12 minutes, remove from the oven, and cool before removing from pan. Makes about a dozen cookies.

(Amber's note: This recipe is gluten free, but if the cookies are too runny, then add 1 tablespoon of flour, tapioca flour or corn starch—the last two being gluten-free options.)

JUDY VAN HEYST

Great-Grandmother's Welsh Cookies

In 1945 these Welsh cookies were my favorites. During this last year of World War II, my family lived in Olathe, Kansas, where my father was stationed at the Naval Air Base. Instead of living on the base, my family was able to rent an unused farmhouse on a 350-acre horse-corn farm.

The old farmhouse had much to be desired, but to a twelve-year-old city girl, it was perfect. To get water pumped to about 100 yards from the house, the windmill way out in the field had to be turned on in the morning and off in the evening. Wood stoves were the heating and cooking sources. Refrigeration was provided by lowering a bucket down into an abandoned well. The outhouse finished off the necessaries.

My mother made these cookies, from a recipe she inherited from her grandmother, on the kitchen wood stove grill—that is, when we had enough sugar and shortening, which were in short supply due to the war. These cookies can also be made like pancakes on a camping grill.

Judy Van Heyst, a friend of SOMOS, is an artist living in El Prado, New Mexico. She and her husband retired here from Pennsylvania eleven years ago. Judy's mother's family was from Scranton, Pennsylvania.

WELSH COOKIES

3 cups all-purpose flour
2 teaspoons baking powder
1/2 teaspoon salt
1 teaspoon nutmeg
1 egg
1 cup sugar
1 cup shortening
1 cup dry currants, soaked in boiling water to plump, then drained

Mix flour, baking powder, salt and nutmeg in a large bowl. Mix egg, sugar and softened shortening in a small bowl. Combine wet and dry ingredients and add soaked currants. Roll out on a floured board and cut into 2-inch circles (you can use a small juice glass). Place on a hot ungreased griddle and brown on both sides (like pancakes). Makes 6 dozen, 2-inch rounds.

Zeppole

I learned to make Zeppole the night Charlie died. I was sixteen years old, my boyfriend Donny was coming to take me to Christmas Eve midnight services, and Charlie was my canary. I'd named him after a cute 1950s TV singer, Charlie Applewhite. I couldn't take my canary for a walk on our New York City sidewalks, but he warbled cheerfully from his cage every day, making us all feel happy for a brief time.

My mother baked Neopolitan sweets every holiday. It had been a long day of baking. Tables held plates of cookies and pretty pyramids of Struffoli and Zeppoli dripping with honey, decorated with candy sprinkles. Heavy frying pans were cooling on the stove when Charlie escaped from his cage. Not used to free flying, he landed in a pan of still-hot Crisco oil. We cleaned him off with tea towels, but he succumbed.

Then Donny arrived. Through tears I told him that I'd left the cage door open and now Charlie was dead. Perplexed momentarily, Donny finally understood, provided sympathy all around and took me away. My mother cleaned the kitchen and my father disposed of the body. Returning home with Christmas magic and adolescent love in our eyes, Donny and I found hot tea and Zeppole waiting for us. They were delicious.

Lorraine Lener Ciancio writes, takes pictures, knits, and likes baking more than cooking. In her next life she wants to be a pastry chef. She writes a blog called The Knitorialist and is editor of the annual SOMOS anthology, *Chokecherries*.

1 cup water

1/2 cup (1 stick) unsalted butter, cut into 1/2 inch cubes

1 teaspoon salt

1 tablespoon sugar

1-1/4 cups all purpose unbleached flour, sifted

4 large eggs

Vegetable oil, such as canola (for frying)

Good-quality honey

Candy sprinkles for decoration

Bring 1 cup water, butter, 1 teaspoon salt, and 1 tablespoon sugar to a boil in a heavy medium saucepan, stirring until butter melts. Add flour to mixture and stir until dough forms ball. Transfer dough to medium bowl. Beat dough (by hand or electric mixer) until crumbly, about 1 minute. Add eggs one at a time, blending well between additions to form smooth dough.

Working in batches, scoop rounded tablespoons of dough into hot (350- degree) oil, turning frequently, until puffed and golden brown on all sides. With a slotted spoon, transfer to paper towels to drain well. Cool slightly. Drizzle with good honey. Shape dough balls into a pyramid on a pretty plate. Scatter colored candy sprinkles over the top, then drizzle with more honey. Makes 30 to 40 memorable Italian treats.

JOHN HAMILTON

Overnight Wonder: A Christmas "Miracle"

Christmas was just not officially Christmas in the Hamilton household until parents and children had collaborated in performing the annual minor family food "miracle."

Once the ritual Christmas Eve viewing of the movie classic "The Christmas Story" had been concluded, Hamilton family "elves" immediately assembled in the kitchen for the collaborative creation of a culinary gem. The combined skills of the entire family were eagerly brought to bear in a tour de force joining family members across generations and over the years.

Children handled the basics, eagerly placing pecans and frozen pastry pieces in the special pan. Parents poured the melted mixture, topping off the Christmas creation. With anticipation rivaling Santa's arrival, this creation was delivered to the overnight magic of a cold oven.

Christmas morning found child and parent alike peering through the glass oven door to witness the soaring heights to which the mixture had been transformed. The oven's heat added a final golden-brown finishing touch. Christmas could now officially begin.

John Hamilton and his wife Peggy retired to Taos and have embraced the Taos experience, including enjoying SOMOS events.

1/2 cup broken pecan pieces

18 frozen dinner rolls, cut in half

1 stick butter (plus butter for greasing pan)

1 box butterscotch pudding (not instant)

1/2 cup brown sugar, packed

1/2 teaspoon ground cinnamon

Partially thaw frozen dinner rolls for 45 minutes, then cut in half with scissors. Combine butter, pudding mix, brown sugar and cinnamon in a small saucepan. Over medium heat, bring to a boil and cook until sugar is dissolved and mixture is smooth.

While the pudding mixture is cooking, butter a tube or Bundt pan well. Layer broken pecan pieces in the bottom of the pan and then cover with dinner roll pieces. Pour pudding mix over frozen rolls and pecans. Cover pan loosely with aluminum foil and place pan in cold oven overnight. Put a sheet pan or heavy-duty aluminum foil on the rack below to catch drips.

In the morning, without opening the oven, turn heat to 325 degrees and bake. After 15 minutes, remove foil. Check after an additional 25 minutes. Remove from oven when top is golden brown, approximately 45 minutes total time (or less at lower altitudes). Let sit in pan for 5 to 10 minutes. Place a large serving plate over the pan and carefully invert. Makes 6 to 8 servings.

BYOB (Beverages)

Lemon Crush.

1 tbr ora...
2 l Sugar
... citric acid
rin... and juice of. 4 lem...
1 ¼ litres boiling wate...

Put the sugar, citric
lemon juice and thin
rind in a saucepa...
on the boiling
over low heat
dissolve... Bri...
boiling point.
leave to coo...
...lized b...

191

KATHLEEN FERGUSON-HUNTINGTON

Arabic Coffee

It's 8:39 a.m. on the fifteenth day of the holy month of Ramadan, in the year 2009, in Al-Jazeera Land. The infidel university professor is speeding along the main thoroughfare heading to teach her morning class at Virginia Commonwealth University, Qatar.

Suddenly she comes upon a slow moving Bentley, weaving dangerously on the road. The driver, she thinks, must be a fasting Muslim with a real blood sugar low. Best to pass him and be out of harm's way. She passes him, giving him a momentary glance.

What she saw appalled her. The driver was reading the Koran, propped up on his steering wheel, as he drove. If he'd died in an accident while reading the Holy Book, she thought, he would surely be transported straight to a heavenly place where seventy-two virgins awaited him.

When she reached her destination, she needed a good cup of coffee.

Kathleen Ferguson-Huntington is a member of SOMOS and a visual artist who taught at a university design school in Qatar before moving back to Taos in 2012.

3 cups water

3 tablespoons ground, lightly roasted coffee

1-1/2 teaspoons ground green cardamom seeds

Bring the water to a boil. Add the ground coffee and boil 10 to 12 minutes. Remove from the heat. Add the ground cardamom seeds, stir, and return to heat to boil 3 more minutes. Allow to sit for about 5 minutes so the grounds settle to the bottom. Pour into an Arabic coffee pot *(dallah)* and drink from a small handle-less cup. Makes 1 to 2 servings.

JEAN E. STEVENS

Life-Changing Smoothies

It was 1967, the year I graduated from high school. It was the summer of Sergeant Pepper's Lonely Hearts Club Band and Strawberry Fields Forever. It was also the year I tasted my first smoothie. Little did I know it would change my life.

Within a year I was working at one of the nation's first smoothie bars located within a Huntington Beach, California, surf shop. It was the dawn of a food revolution, the era of *The Whole Earth Catalog*.

Later, a high school friend's mom opened the Sunshine Juice Bar in Laguna Beach. It was the healthy place to be when George Harrison took a smoothie break during a 1970 Christmas rock concert.

And it was during that time that I made date shakes and smoothies while working at the Orange Inn overlooking the Pacific Ocean. It was truly the era of "California Dreaming."

Now, almost a half century later, I begin my day making smoothies—one for my ailing mother and one for me. Mine gives me great energy. A Taos nurse claims they extend my mother's life.

Jean E. Stevens, an instructor of Art History at UNM-Taos, is also a filmmaker, screenwriter, multi-media artist and SOMOS member.

ORANGE BLISS SMOOTHIE

4-5 freshly squeezed Valencia oranges (about 2 cups orange juice)
2 bananas
1-2 cups strawberries (or seasonal fruit like papaya, blueberries)
1/4 cup almonds
1 tablespoon fresh, peeled, chopped ginger
1/4 cup whey protein powder
(Optional: cinnamon to taste)

Blend all of the ingredients together. Makes 3 servings.

VALERIE MILLER

Booga Booga Smoothie

A few years ago, a wonderful and vivacious woman in my neighborhood invited me to join her on an early morning hike in the mountains behind our homes. As time passed, more neighbors participated, and the trails became more varied and longer. Friendships have developed, and you can now find groups of us in the mountains most days, with hikes lasting up to two hours.

After hiking, I would frequently feel drained. One of my hiking buddies suggested that if I ate something beforehand, I would have more energy throughout the day. Made sense to me! So I experimented and finally came up with a healthy, low-calorie smoothie.

From just after Easter until Thanksgiving, my weekday mornings typically begin shortly after 5 a.m. with the chance to sit down and connect with my husband while we share a smoothie. I walk out the door a little before 6 and return home around 8 a.m.

Great friends, great spouse, a great hike, good nourishment. My day now starts well, and I come home feeling refreshed physically and mentally. What could be better than that?

Valerie Miller, a friend of SOMOS and an avid hiker, lives in Taos.

196

1 small, ripe banana

1 cup fresh fruit (be creative: berries, pineapple, kiwi, mango...)

1/4 cup orange juice

1/4 cup light coconut milk

1 cup nonfat yogurt

Sweetener to taste

2 tablespoons coarsely ground flax seed

Place all but the flax seed in a blender and blend until smooth. Add flax seed and blend a few seconds more. Depending on the fruit and sweetener (I use a packet of stevia), the calorie count is about 200 per serving. Makes 2 servings.

(Valerie's note: I named my smoothie Booga Booga after our current favorite hiking trail. Also, when my bananas start getting a little too ripe, I make up "kits" of the fruit [minus the yogurt and sweetener] and freeze them. I take one out of the freezer the night before, and by morning it's slushy and easier to blend.)

Authors & Their Stories Index

Authors & Their Stories Index

Recipe Index

Recipe Index

MAGPIE'S BEADS

Mag Dimond

The Magpie creates wildly inventive necklaces using ancient beads and talismans,
contemporary and Venetian glass, carved polymer, and semi-precious stones.
magpiesbeads.com

Hotel La Fonda de Taos

The oldest hotel in Taos. Experience Taos history in the only hotel on Taos Plaza.
Nineteen rooms, five suites, and the penthouse offer modern amenities.
575-758-2211, lafondataos.com

Taos Pizza Out Back

Voted "Best Pizza in Taos, 2012." A local favorite and a destination for visitors.
Pastas, salads, soups, kids menu, beer & wine. Open daily at 11:00am.
575-758-3112, taospizzaoutback.com

Sponsors

3: A Taos Press

A multicultural publisher dedicated to
honoring and fostering our poets' voices.
3taospress.com

**Dan Cassidy Studio
& Gallery**

Dan Cassidy Studio

Fine art photographer and printmaker.
taosbritdan.4ormat.com

Antonio's A Taste of Mexico

Serving contemporary and traditional
cuisine from select regions of Mexico.
antoniosoftaos.com

Dreamcatcher B & B Inn

Your "home away from home" in Taos.
575-758-0613, dreambb.com

Cid's Food Market

The best selection of organic
and local foods in Taos.
cidsfoodmarket.com

The Enchanted Florist

High-quality fresh cut flowers
with superior design for 20 years.
taosflorist.com

Sponsors

Taos Travel & Artours
Custom travel arrangements
anywhere in the world.
575-758-4246

Taoswebb
A visitor's guide to Taos
and Northern New Mexico.
taoswebb.com

Webb Design, Inc
Design and marketing for the tourism
industry and fine arts arena.
webbdesigninc.com

IN-KIND DONATIONS

Bonnie Lee Black

Linda Michel-Cassidy

Dan Cassidy Studio

Lorraine Lener Ciancio

Barbara Scott
finaleyes.net

FEEL Design Associates
Inspired graphic design
for print and the web.
feeldesignassociates.com

Geraint Smith Photography Gallery
Photo tours and workshops,
fine art photography.
geraintsmith.com

Nighthawk Press
P.O. Box 1222 • Taos, NM 87571

Welcome to the **Taos** Farmers Market

Aprons...$25   Tshirts!
Caps.....$20   Mens...$12
                 Womens.$15
Hoodies..$40 25 Kids...$12
Baskets.$30   Organic
Tote bags.$20   mens $20

follow
US